Just Show Me
Which Button to Click!
Computer training for busy people

PEGGY DUNCAN

PSC
PRESS

ATLANTA, GEORGIA

Just show me which button to click!

Publisher's Cataloging-in-Publication (Provided by Quality Books, Inc.)

Duncan, Peggy.
    Just show me which button to click! : computer
training for busy people / written by Peggy
Duncan. ~ 1st ed.
    p. cm.
    Includes index.
    LCCN: 99-91133
    ISBN: 0-9674728-0-6

    1. Computers.   2. Electronic data processing.
3. Microsoft software.   I. Title.

QA76.D86 2000   004
                      QBI99-1658

Book created in Microsoft® Word 97. Screen captures made with Paint Shop Pro 5 by Jasc Software, Inc.

Cover design by Chris Handley Graphic Design, Inc., Atlanta, GA.
Logo design for Duncan Resource Group, Inc., by Ashley Davis Designs, Atlanta, GA.
Cover photo by Philip McCollum Photography, Atlanta, GA.

Trademarks

Just Show Me
Which Button to Click!

To my son, **Steven**, and his son, **Christopher**.
The first time I heard "Grandma" was a very
quiet moment for me.

Acknowledgments

By **God's** grace, I am able to persevere.

A most special thanks to **Maurice Threatt,** who was so patient throughout this process. He calls me a little machine, and is so proud of me.

Thanks also to my Mom, **Verta Haskins,** and my baby brother, **Thurman "Bud" Spicer, Jr.,** who have always had to put up with me. Starting my business was easier as you stood by ready to feed me.

And with special gratitude, I have to thank four of my good buddies: **Kim Joyner, Patty Mabra, Michael Fields,** and **Cedrick Prather,** who helped me through all this.

I also wish to thank **Brad Lightner,** my business advisor and my dear friend, who guided me from the very beginning, and who always found the time.

I wish to also acknowledge some of my very first clients who had enough faith in me to hire me, and who never stopped supporting me.

Dr. Robert J. Yancy	**Dr. Robyn Levy**
James Dallas	**Curley Dossman, Jr.**
Jackie Steele	**Art Robinson, Jr.**
Harriette Watkins	**Dr. Janis Coombs Reid**

Finally, I have to thank **John Rasor** and all my other friends at Georgia-Pacific Corporation who helped make my dream a reality.

How to Contact the Author

Peggy Duncan provides consulting services to businesses looking to make work easier for their staff and to individuals seeking to increase their efficiency. By providing her clients with the tools they need to get organized, streamline business processes, and make better use of technology, Peggy not only gives her clients a competitive edge, but helps them free up time to enjoy their lives more fully.

Requests for information about her services, as well as inquiries about her availability for seminars or computer classes, should be directed to the address below. If you have a comment or idea for this book, you are also encouraged to contact her.

Peggy Duncan c/o PSC Press
1010 Pine Tree Trail, Suite 300
Atlanta, GA 30349-4979
770-991-1316
eMail: pscpress@mindspring.com

Computer classes based on this book can be arranged at your company site. For more information, visit Peggy at:

www.duncanresource.com

TABLE OF CONTENTS-WORD

WORD

Contents   Word

WORD

WORD

TABLE OF CONTENTS-EXCEL

EXCEL

TABLE OF CONTENTS-POWERPOINT

POWERPOINT

POWERPOINT

TABLE OF CONTENTS-WINDOWS

WINDOWS

Preface

This book started out being a computer manual for Peggy to use in her training classes. Her students loved its format and content so much, she decided to dress it up and make it available to you.

Peggy's students often commented that other books they had found were too overwhelming and just too big to tackle. Realizing that few business people would ever read and study those big, thick computer manuals the way she does, Peggy set out to create a simple guide that makes everything as easy as possible. Not a lot of pages—just quick, step-by-step instructions and pictures that will increase your computer know-how overnight.

Best of all, *Just Show Me Which Button to Click! "Computer Training for Busy People"* is loaded with beginning to advanced features that Peggy uses every day to save herself time. So, you can be sure Peggy's system works!

It's not enough to have the technology— you have to know what it can do and how to do it. Yet, if you don't take classes beyond the basics or read manuals or visit Help, how will you ever know?

I think the pages of this book offer the perfect solution!

Introduction

This book is for busy people. For people who want to make the most of their on-the-job hours, so they can make the most of their off-the-job lives. For people who know there must be a better way to use their computer, but who haven't found out what that way is. For people who have bought computer books in the past, only to turn them into dust collectors.

Just Show Me Which Button to Click! will enable you to become more comfortable with your software. In no time, you'll find yourself being more adventurous at the keyboard. Trying new things, clicking different buttons and keys to see what happens. And not being intimidated by any of it!

How to Use this Book

Each software title is contained in its own chapter with a separate table of contents. A separate index for each chapter is located in the back of the book.

If you're new to the Windows environment, or if you still get baffled over where your document went when you saved it, start with the Windows chapter near the back of the book. If after Windows you still feel a little intimidated by it all, go through the PowerPoint chapter. PowerPoint is fun and really easy to learn. Learning it will give you a quick boost to your self-confidence. Then, you'll be ready to breeze through Word or Excel.

How Content is Arranged

Information is grouped to resemble the layout of the software's Menu Bar. For example:

If a feature works the same in Word (the first chapter) as it does in other software, instructions for it are not repeated in the subsequent chapters.

Steps are often separated by a /. At times, you'll notice that some instructions on using a feature will stop before you finish the task. This is because the next step should be very obvious to you. Also, please realize that changes made in subsequent editions of the software could result in slight variations in the dialog boxes.

To get the latest update of your software, visit the Microsoft Web site for free downloads at www.microsoft.com, and click Downloads. Once in the Download Center, click the Product Name drop-down arrow, and choose the appropriate edition of Office 97 you need to update.

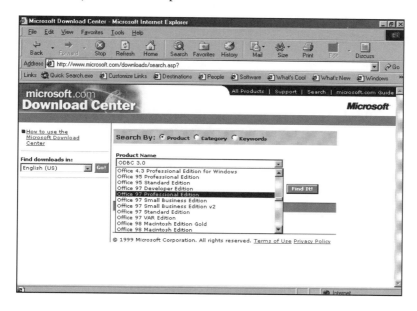

On rare occasions, you'll be referred to Help for more details on a feature. In this case, it's because there are so many options available for that feature that mentioning them all in a fast-paced book like this is simply not feasible. Then again, clicking Help will give you a chance to familiarize yourself with how to find additional answers in Help.

Help Using Windows

If you are not familiar with the Windows environment or are new to technology, you'll find the bonus chapter on Windows to be very helpful. Located in the back of this book, it has the help you'll need to manage your files. You'll also find the book that comes with the Windows software extremely helpful.

Also, you have tools right on your computer that can help—your Windows® 98 CD. The Windows software comes with an excellent tutorial that explains computer terminology you may not be familiar with, as well as demonstrations on how to use your mouse, how to double-click, and so much more.

Let's Get Started

Okay, that's all I have to say. Now it's your turn to get started. Your turn to stop stumbling through your software, taking too long to finish simple tasks. Learn it. Play with it. Use it. You'll soon find that there's more to this stuff than making something bold and changing its size.

As a freelance marketer and copywriter, the faster I can complete a job, the more profitable it becomes. This book will boost my productivity—and my bottom line.

David Schwartz
Alexandria, VA

Just Show Me Which Button to Click!

WORD 97

GETTING STARTED

The Word Screen

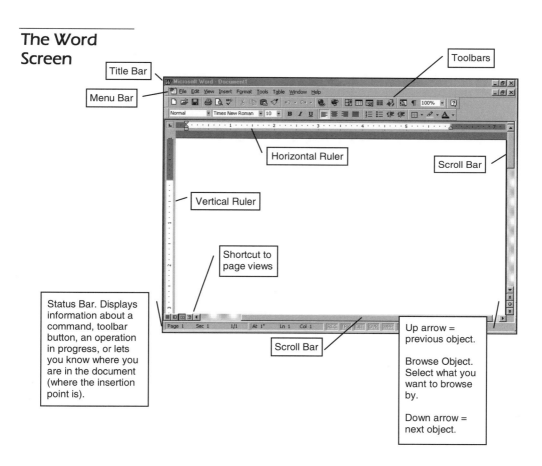

Title Bar

Menu Bar

Toolbars

Horizontal Ruler

Scroll Bar

Vertical Ruler

Shortcut to page views

Status Bar. Displays information about a command, toolbar button, an operation in progress, or lets you know where you are in the document (where the insertion point is).

Scroll Bar

Up arrow = previous object.

Browse Object. Select what you want to browse by.

Down arrow = next object.

Toolbar Buttons

Guess what? Those little toolbar buttons aren't just there to make the screen colorful. Clicking them makes things happen. Hold your mouse pointer under each one, and the tool tip will let you know what its function is.

Browse Object

One part of the screen that you might not be familiar with is the Browse Object feature. It allows you to select how you want Word to browse through your document.

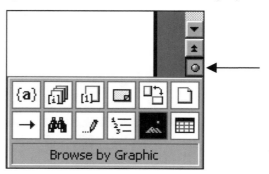

If you want to look for each graphic in your document:

1. Click the Browse Object to display browsing options.
2. Click the graphic browser. Using the arrow buttons on the scroll bar, go to the next or previous graphic.
3. Click another browser type when finished.

Navigation

There are several ways to move quickly through your document.

- Press Ctrl+Home to go to the top of the document.
- Press Ctrl+End to go to bottom of a document.
- Press the End key to go to end of a line.
- Press the Home key to go to start of a line.
- Press Page Up or Page Down keys to move up or down on a page.
- Press Ctrl+G to go to a certain page.
- Drag scroll bars to go up or down on a page.
- Create hyperlinks so you can "jump" from one place in your document to another (or to another document).

FILE

New Document

By default, Word opens with a page of an unnamed document in view. To create a document when no page is available:

1. Click the New button on the Standard toolbar.

Open a Document

To open a previously created document:

1. Click the Open button on the Standard toolbar.

Clicking the Open button takes you to a dialog box that will allow you to browse through your files to find the one you want. You can preview the document before you open it to make sure it's the right one.

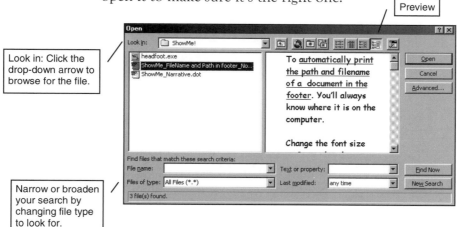

Preview

Look in: Click the drop-down arrow to browse for the file.

Narrow or broaden your search by changing file type to look for.

Note: *To look for a recently opened document, click File, look toward the bottom of the menu box/click desired file to open.*

Save a File

When you have finished your document (or as you're working on it), and you want to save it:

1. Click the Save button/click the Save in drop-down arrow to browse for the folder in which you want to save the document/double-click the folder to open it.

2. Name the file/click the Save as type drop-down arrow, and click the desired file type/click Save.

3. **Or,** click File/Save/repeat same steps as above.

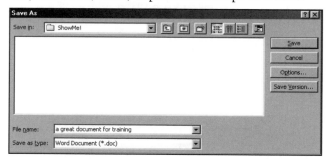

Note: *Clicking the Save button is a quick way to save your changes as you work.*

Create New Folder

While in Explore, if you find that you need to create a new folder in which to save a document, you can do so from the Save As dialog box by clicking the New Folder toolbar button. (Refer to the *Windows* chapter if you need more help with creating new folders.)

Save As

If you are working in a previously saved document, and you want to create a completely different file while leaving the original file intact, click File/Save As. Steps for saving the document are the same as above. If you're saving the file to a diskette, typing a: in front of the file name will do it.

WORD

Revert to Previous Version of Document

If you open a saved document, work on it and ruin it, you can revert to the previously saved version.

1. While the ruined document is open, click the Open toolbar button/find the name of the file that is already open and double-click it to open it again/click "Yes" when asked if you want to revert to the previously saved version.

Closing a Document

1. Either click the window control button (the X); press Ctrl+W; or click File/Close.

Note: To close multiple open documents, hold down the Shift key/click File/Close All.

Page Setup

1. Click File/Page Setup. From here, you can change the margins, page size, and layout.

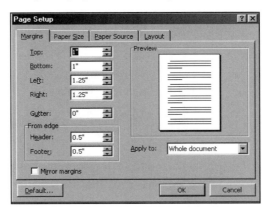

Margins

By changing the Apply to box, you can change the margins and apply the change to the entire document, selected sections, or "from this point forward," depending on where you are in your document.

Mirror Margins	Mirror margins are used when you're printing pages on both sides of the paper, and the pages will face each other as in this book. (The right and left margins become inside and outside margins.) Word mirrors the margins and places a binding gutter between the two pages.
	You can leave more room for the binding of the book by increasing the gutter.

Print Options

Changing Options

1. Click Tools/Options/click the Print tab/click your preferences/click OK to close.

Printing Intermittent Pages

1. Click File/Print/Pages/type in text box as below/click OK.

   ▤ 1-2, 4-7 to print pages 1 and 2, then 4 through 7.

   ▤ 13- to print from page 13 to end of document.

   ▤ s1-s3 to print sections 1 through 3.

To print the current page you're working on:

1. Click File/Print/Current page/OK.

Quick Print

If you have no need to change print options, you can click the Print toolbar button to bypass the Print dialog box.

Properties

To view document properties such as its file location, word count, etc., from inside your document:

1. Click File/Properties/click to view each tab.

Templates

A template is a collection of formatting, page settings, font attributes, text, and other information. When you create a new document, all the attributes in the selected template are copied into the new document.

Every document you create is based on some type of template. You can create your own, or use one of the many built-in templates that come with Word.

1. To create a template, click File/New/choose the template you want to base your new document on (if any)/click the Create New Template option (directly above the Cancel button)/click OK.

Or create a regular document, and save it as a template.

1. Create the document/click File/Save As/name your template.

2. Change document type to .dot by clicking the Save as type drop-down arrow and choosing the .dot extension. Word will take you to your default template location as explained on page 10.

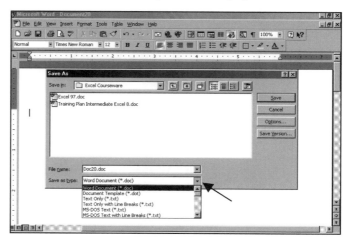

Normal Template

The default template for Word documents is called the Normal template (a copy of this template comes up when you click the New button to start a new document), and it is stored in your default template location. If you want to make changes to this default template, locate your Word templates.

To find out where your templates are stored (where Word points to when you click File/New):

1. Click Tools/Options/click the File Locations tab, and note the location next to User Templates.

Once you find your Templates folder, double-click it to open. The Normal template should be located here.

1. Right-click the normal.dot file/click Open.
2. Here, change your default font size to 12, change the typeface, etc./close the document, and save (now you won't have to change your type size to 12 every time you create a new document).

A shortcut to changing the font of the Normal template (from inside any document based on it) is as follows:

1. Click Format/Font/make your changes/click the Default button (bottom, left-hand corner)/close and click "Yes" to save changes to the Normal template.

Word's Built-In Templates

To use Word's built-in templates to create a document:

1. Click File/New/double-click your choice.

A **copy** of the template is opened. Create your document as you normally would.

Changing Template

Once you create a base template, you'll start to create documents based on that template as just explained. Changes you make to this **copy** of the template **don't affect** the original template, and will only be in effect for the document you're presently working in. To change the template, you have to open it and change it (as you did for the normal template). This confuses a lot of people, so make sure this is clear.

Right-Clicking

Pressing the right mouse button displays a shortcut menu. The shortcuts listed in the menu change according to what you were doing when you right-clicked. For example, if you're working in a table and right-click on it, table-related shortcuts will appear.

Send To

You can use a shortcut to send your document via fax, eMail, etc., depending on what you have installed on your computer.

1. Click File/point to Send To/click your choice.

Note: *The first time you use the Send To Mail Recipient feature, have your eMail program running in the background so Word will know which eMail program you use.*

Print Preview

Preview your document before printing it to see how it looks on the page.

1. Click the Print Preview button on your Standard toolbar. Your mouse pointer will become a magnifier.

Once you're in Print Preview, you can zoom in on a particular part of your page.

2. Hold the magnifier (the mouse pointer) over the section you want to zoom in on, and click.

If you want to edit your document *while in Print Preview*:

3. Click the magnifier on the Print Preview toolbar. It will turn into an I-beam so you can edit. Click Close Preview button when finished.

To view one or multiple pages at once:

4. Click the Multiple Pages button, and drag it to see more pages.

5. Click the One Page button to see a single page.

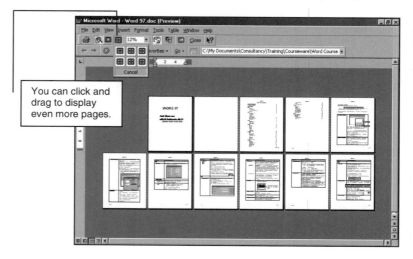

You can click and drag to display even more pages.

EDIT

Cut-Copy-Paste

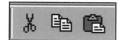

You can Cut or Copy text or graphics from your document, and paste it somewhere else.

1. Select the text or graphic, and click either Cut or Copy. The item will reside on the clipboard until you cut or copy something else on top of it.

2. Click the desired target location, and click Paste.

Undo/Redo

Correct mistakes up to 100 actions. You can Undo/Redo one action at the time or several at once.

> Click the drop-down arrow to see multiple actions. You can select several actions and Undo all at once. The same goes for Redo.
>
> You can't skip around.

Drag-and-Drop Editing

Moving/copying text with the mouse:

1. Select the text you want to **move**.

2. Hold the mouse pointer over the selected text, and click and drag it to its new location (the dotted line indicates where text will land once mouse is released).

To **copy** text to another location:

1. Select the text you want to **copy and move**.

2. While holding the mouse pointer over the selected text, press Ctrl, then click and drag text to its new location (you'll see a + sign to indicate you're copying instead of moving).

Find-Replace-Go To

Locate all instances of words/phrases and change them.

1. To find it, click Edit/Find (or Ctrl+F)/type text in the Find what box/click Find Next.

2. To find it and replace it with something else, click Edit/Replace (or Ctrl+H)/ type text in both the Find what box and the Replace with box/click Replace or Replace All.

3. To find a specific page, click Edit/Go To (or Ctrl+G).

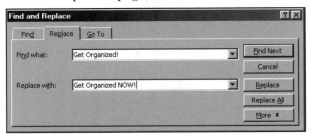

Note: *Double-clicking on the left-hand side of the Status Bar is a shortcut to Go To.*

Paste Special

If you want to include information from one document (source) into a new document (target), and you want the target document to be updated automatically every time you edit the source document, you can paste the information as a link (into the target).

Pasting Links

Example: You have your resume (a file named My Resume) that you send out attached to different documents. Instead of copying and pasting your resume into your document the regular way, paste it as a link.

1. Copy source document to the clipboard/open target/click where you want source document to go/click Edit/Paste Special/Paste Link.

Note: *To change the linked file, go back to the source document.*

Pasting Text Unformatted

If you want to paste information into your document, and you want the information to come in with the formatting of the document you're working in, paste the text as unformatted.

To paste text as unformatted:

1. Copy the text you want to insert/go back to the document you were working in/click where you want to paste new information/click Edit/Paste Special/Unformatted text.

Return to Place of Last Edit

To return to where you left off the last time you edited a document:

1. Open the document/press Shift+F5.

Note: Pressing this command repeatedly lets you jump to the last three places you edited, even if one of the places is in another open document.

Repeat Most Actions

Pressing F4 (or Ctrl+Y) will repeat *most* actions.

1. Type some text/press F4. Text will retype.

Non-Breaking Hyphens

To keep words or phone numbers with hyphens together, make the hyphen non-breaking:

1. Press Ctrl+Shift+hyphen to create a non-breaking hyphen.

Non-Breaking Spaces

To keep words with spaces between them together (like your name), make the space non-breaking:

1. Press Ctrl+Shift+spacebar to create a non-breaking space.

Selecting Text

Before you can format a word, paragraph, graphic, etc., you have to select it first so the software will know which item it is to work on. The item will appear to be highlighted in most cases.

One word. Click once inside the word, **or** double-click it.

Sentence. Press Ctrl, and click anywhere in the sentence.

Paragraph. Triple-click anywhere in the paragraph, **or** if you're not in a table, click the selection bar (the blank space outside the left margin. The mouse pointer will turn into a large, white arrow that points inward).

Entire document. Press Ctrl+A, **or** triple-click the selection bar described above.

Vertical Text. Hold down the Alt key, then click and drag across and straight down as in a column with the mouse (doesn't work inside a table).

Block of text. Click where you want the selection to start, then hold the Shift key down, and click where you want the selection to end.

From certain point in a document to the end. Click where you want the selection to begin, then press Ctrl+Shift+End. From the first click to the end of the document will become selected.

VIEW

Page Views

Page Layout. Shows exact page layout as it will print. This view uses more memory, and scrolling is slower.

Normal. Hides left-hand ruler and graphics. Editing and moving through the document is faster.

Outline. Shows document in outline format. Makes rearranging document easier.

Full Screen. Removes toolbars and rulers so you can see as much of the screen as possible. Great for straight typing of manuscripts.

Master Document. If you work with large documents, you may want to refer to the Suggested Reading in the back of this book for a reference book with details on this feature. Master documents allow you to work with your document in smaller pieces called subdocuments.

You can change the views of your page:

1. Click View/click on the desired view.

Or, use the shortcut tools in the lower, left corner of the bottom scroll bar.

Zoom Page

Increase the percentage of the zoom so you can see more detail on your page.

Header and Footer

When you want text to appear on every page, put it in the header or footer.

1. Click View/Header and Footer/click inside the header/type and format tex (or click appropriate button on the Header and Footer toolbar to insert date, time, etc.).

2. On the Switch Between Header and Footer toolbar button, click Switch to Footer/type desired text/click Close on the Header and Footer toolbar.

Different Layout of Headers and Footers

Word first creates headers and footers the same for the entire document. However, if you've created sections in your document, you can have a different header and footer on each page, or on a group of pages.

If you're working on a report that will print on both sides of the paper and the pages will face each other (as in this book), you will want the even page numbers to print on the left-hand side of the page and the odd page numbers to print on the right-hand side.

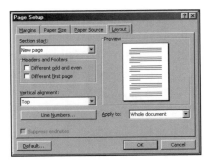

The following page explains how you can create different headers and footers within the same document.

Managing Different Headers and Footers

In your document, first create a title page. Then:

1. Click View/Header and Footer.

2. From inside the header or footer box/click the Page Setup button on the Header and Footer toolbar/click Different First Page on the Layout tab/Apply to the Whole Document/click OK.

3. Leave the header and footer blank for the first page of the document, and click Close on the Header and Footer toolbar.

4. After the last line of text on the title page, click Insert/Break/Section breaks to start the rest of your document on the next page/click OK.

   You have to insert a section break instead of a regular page break because you want to format the two sections independently (one section will have no header or footer, and the second section will).

5. On this new page, repeat instructions to get back to the Header/click the Same as Previous button to unlink this section header from the previous one (because in this case, you want the header of the section you're in to be different from the header of the previous section).

6. Type the desired text for the header/Switch to Footer / click the Same as Previous button to unlink from the previous section/type desired text for the footer/click Close.

7. Repeat steps 5 and 6 for each new section. (You don't need to insert section breaks when subsequent pages will have the same header and footer.)

Toolbars-Customizing

You can customize your toolbar to house different buttons you use a lot.

Example: If you type a lot of envelopes, instead of clicking Tools/Envelopes and Labels, just drag Word's built-in toolbar button for envelopes to your toolbar.

1. Click View/point to Toolbars/click Customize (**or** right-click anywhere on a toolbar, and click Customize).

2. Click the Commands tab.

3. In the left window, find the Category you want (in Word, the Envelope Command is under Tools, so this is the Category you look for here).

4. In the right window, find the Envelopes Command.

5. Click the Envelopes Command, drag it to your toolbar and drop it. An I-beam pointer will indicate where your new button will land. Put it somewhere that's logical for you.

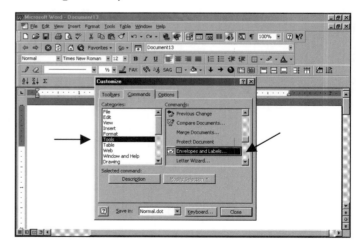

Now, every time you need to create envelopes or labels, just click your new toolbar button.

Toolbars-Creating

You can also create your own toolbar to house commands that you don't use often enough to display all the time.

1. Right-click on any toolbar/click Customize/Toolbars tab/New.

2. Give the toolbar a name/decide on the template or document in which you want it to appear/click OK. (You'll see what looks like a portion of a toolbar.)

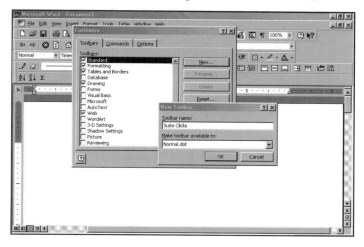

3. Click the Commands tab/click a Category in the left window (as explained in the section on Toolbars-Customizing)/click the desired Command/drag it to the new toolbar and drop it.

Note: *You can change the face of a toolbar button while the Customize dialog box is open. On your new toolbar, right-click on the button you want to change/click in the Name box and rename it/click off the shortcut menu/continue with steps below.*

4. Repeat steps to add other commands to your new toolbar.

5. Close the toolbar, or drag it to join your others.

**Toolbars-
Displaying**

You can display or hide your choice of toolbars.

1. Click View/point to Toolbars/click desired toolbar.
2. Or, right-click on any toolbar, and click your choice.

INSERT

Page Break

1. Press Ctrl+Enter to force a page break.

Section Break

Breaking your document into sections allows you to format pages independently.

If you want the different sections to continue on the same page, make it a continuous section break.

If you have different even and odd pages, you can create a section break that will make the next text you type land on either.

To insert a section break in your document:

1. Click Insert/Break/choose desired type of Section break/click OK.

Text Box

If you insert your graphic or text inside a text box, you can control how text wraps around it and how it falls on the page.

1. Display the Drawing toolbar/click the Text Box toolbar button (the mouse pointer turns into a cross).

2. Bring the pointer into the body of your document, and click and drag out your text box.

To change the look of the text box:

1. Click the box to select it.

2. Double-click selection box.

3. Change text box options as explained on page 24.

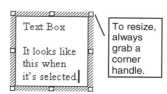

To insert text or a graphic inside a text box, click inside of it and type or paste text from the clipboard, or insert a graphic as described on page 27. *If your graphic places behind the box, see page 97 for instructions on how to change the placement order.*

Note: *While the text box is selected, you can move it in any direction using the keyboard arrow keys.*

Text Box Options

By placing objects inside a text box, you can control how text wraps around it.

1. Double-click the text box/click the Wrapping tab.

   Note: *To get a description of each Wrapping style, hold the mouse pointer over each type and right-click/click What's This.*

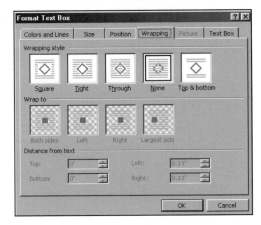

2. To change the Internal Margin (how far the graphic is away from the text box edges), click Text Box tab.

3. If you don't want the lines of the text box to print, click the Colors and Lines tab/click the Line Color drop-down arrow/choose No Line.

4. To change the Fill color or Effects/click the Colors and Lines tab/click the Fill drop-down arrow.

5. To set where the text box appears on the page, click the Position tab. Position the graphic a certain distance from the paragraph, page, or column, both horizontally or vertically.

6. If desired, click **Move Object with text** to move the object up or down on the page as the paragraph changes. And click **Anchor text** to keep the object on the same page as the paragraph it's anchored to.

Linked Text Boxes

Linked text boxes are ideal for creating newsletters and similar documents. With linked text boxes, you can have text flow from a column on one page to a column on a different page. You could have an article start on the first page and flow to a text box on the second page. As you add or delete lines of text, the text reflows automatically.

You can only create links to empty text boxes. Create the text boxes on each page first. Then, you'll create the links between the desired text boxes.

1. Create text boxes that are side-by-side on the first page of your document.

2. Insert a page break, and repeat for all pages.

To create a forward link between two text boxes:

1. Right-click on any edge of the origin text box. The mouse pointer will turn into a cup.

2. Click the cup pointer inside the destination text box.

If you're working in one of the linked text boxes, and you want to quickly go to the other:

1. Right-click on any edge of the text box you're working in/click Next Text Box (or Previous Text Box).

To break the link between the two text boxes:

1. Right-click on any edge of the origin text box/click Break Forward Link.

Note*: To see how linked text boxes work, check out Word's built-in newsletter template. Click File/New/Publications tab/Newsletter Wizard (if installed).*

Insert Page Numbers

You can insert page numbers in the footer or header two ways. One is through the Header and Footer feature as explained on page 18. The other is the Insert Page Numbers feature, which is explained below.

1. Click Insert/Page Numbers/choose the position and alignment/format the number if needed/uncheck Show number on first page box if desired.

Insert File

Sometimes you might want to insert another file into your working document.

1. Click inside your document where you want the new file to appear.

2. Click Insert/File/find the file you want to insert/double-click the file name.

Note: If you insert the file as a link, every time you update the original file (source), the linked file (target) changes automatically. You would follow instructions above, but when you find the file to insert, check the Link to File box (upper, right-hand side of window).

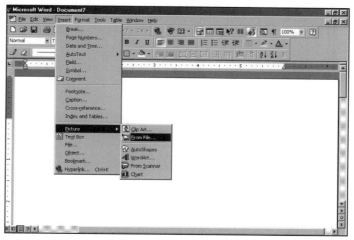 (positioned to the right margin: **WORD**)

Insert Picture

The Insert Picture command lets you insert graphics, clip art, graphs, and so on.

1. Click Insert/point to Picture/click your choice.

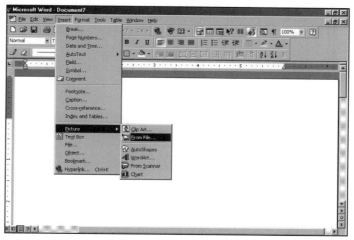

If you want the picture to position itself inline with the text:

1. Right-click the picture/click Format Picture/click the Position tab/uncheck Float over text.

It's a good idea to draw a text box with your Drawing tool and insert the graphic inside the text box. You can then control its placement and how text wraps around it. *(See page 23 for more information on the text box.)*

Insert Excel Worksheet

If you need the power of Excel's formulas in your Word document, you can insert an Excel spreadsheet.

1. Click the Insert Excel Worksheet toolbar button/drag out your columns and rows/enter data/click off worksheet when finished.
2. Later, double-click the spreadsheet to edit it.

Table of Contents (TOC)

Creating a Table of Contents for your document is easy. However, you'll have to understand how Styles are created and their relationship to the Table of Contents.

You can learn about Styles beginning on page 65.

Heading Levels

The Table of Contents is created based on the heading levels inside the document. Looking at the Table of Contents for this section of the book, you'll notice that there are different levels of headings.

The heading levels in this book come in all different sizes, and typefaces. Some are bold, and some are not, etc. The top level (i.e., File, View, etc.) is a Head Level 1. The second level is a Head 2, and so on.

Example:

> **EDIT** is a Head Level 1
>
> **Paste Special** is a Head Level 2
>
> **Pasting Links** is a Head Level 3

In this example, EDIT is the main heading, Paste Special is a subtopic of EDIT, and Pasting Links is a subtopic of Paste Special.

Creating the TOC

1. Create a blank page in front of your document that you created using head levels. Type the title, "Table of Contents" /format the text/space down twice.

    (Make sure you don't have a heading level assigned to this title because it would end up being listed in the TOC.)

2. Click Insert/Index and Tables/click the Table of Contents tab/make your selections/click OK.

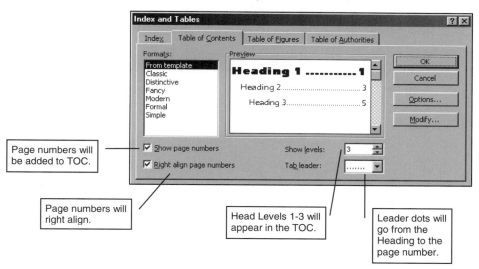

Page numbers will be added to TOC.

Page numbers will right align.

Head Levels 1-3 will appear in the TOC.

Leader dots will go from the Heading to the page number.

Toggle Field Code

A quick way to change the number of heading levels in your TOC is to toggle to the field code that makes it up.

1. Right-click anywhere inside the TOC/click Toggle Field Codes/change the number that depicts the heading levels included in the TOC.

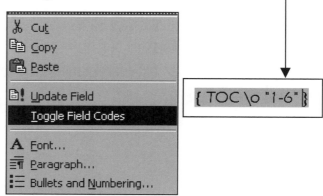

2. Repeat Step 1 to toggle back to the TOC.

Navigating from the Table of Contents

Once the Table of Contents has been created, you can jump to any page in your document just by clicking one of its page numbers. (The same goes for cross-references once you create them later in this chapter.)

Updating the Table of Contents

The Table of Contents will update every time you print the document as long as the Update Fields box is checked on the Print tab under Tools/Options.

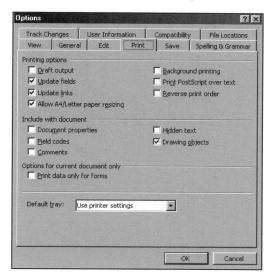

To update the TOC from within your document:

1. Right-click anywhere on the TOC/click Update Field/update page numbers only or the entire table.

Note*: Never update the TOC with the Show/Hide button activated as the page numbers could be thrown off. Also, always update the Table of Contents, even when you make very small changes to your document. Don't learn this lesson the hard way.*

Bookmarks

A Bookmark is a named item, which can be text, a graphic, or a location in your document.

You can bookmark a place in your document the same way you do when using a bookmark in a book you're reading. With the Bookmark in your Word document, you can quickly locate a specific named location.

First, you have to identify the text you want as a Bookmark. Then, you create the Bookmark.

To create a Bookmark:

1. Select the text you want to bookmark.
2. Click Insert/Bookmark/name the Bookmark/click Add.

Note: When naming your bookmark, you can't use spaces, punctuation marks, or other similar character The name can contain up to 40 characters.

To go to the Bookmark later:

1. Press Ctrl+G/click Bookmark in the Go to what box/click the drop-down arrow to locate and click the Bookmark name/press Enter/click Close.

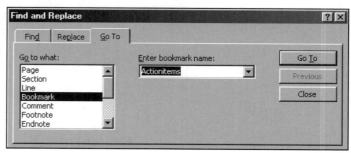

Index

You can easily create an index for your document. Word will find every instance of a word or phrase you specify, mark it as an index entry, and list it in your index, along with the page number(s) on which it's located. As your document changes, the page numbers will update automatically.

The steps in creating an index include:

- Deciding which words or phrases should appear in your index, as well as how they should read.
- Marking words or phrases you want in your index so each index entry is identified with an index field.
- Creating the actual index for your document so you can see how it displays before you continue.
- Creating Bookmarks throughout your document so you'll be able to display page ranges in your index. Then, you'll mark the entries for the Bookmarks.
- Creating appropriate index-style cross-references (i.e., *See also ....* or *See...*).

Wait until your document is finished before creating the index, and be very meticulous in deciding what should be included and how it should appear. This is tedious work, and will probably require a lot of trial and error before you fully understand how it all works (it did for me!).

Review the steps for creating Bookmarks (page 32) and a simple Table (page 87) before you begin.

Until you get used to it, go slowly, and don't try to do too much at one time (i.e., don't try to mark the text, create the Bookmark entry, create the cross-reference—all at once). The instructions here take it one step at a time.

Deciding What Goes in the Index

A good place to start in deciding what goes in your index is the Table of Contents (see page 28). It lists important topics and terms in your document, and shows how they relate to each other. On the other hand, you can just print your document and scan it for entries.

1. In a separate document from the one for which you're creating an index, create a two-column table (see how to create Tables on page 87).

2. In the first column, enter the text you will mark as an index entry. In the second column, type the actual words you want to use to describe this entry. (You can have this text read any way you desire. For example, the second column below could instead read "Creating Headers and Footers.")

3. If you want to include a subentry of Header and Footer in your index, create a second row for this entry. Repeat Header and Footer in the first column, and then rewrite Header and Footer in the second column, followed by a colon: and the subentry text.

Header and Footer	Header and Footer
Header and Footer	Header and Footer: different layouts
Header and Footer	Header and Footer: managing different

The index entry will look like this:

Header and Footer, page no.
different layouts, page no.
managing different, page no.

Note: *Writing it out this way improves consistency when marking the text. It's especially helpful because the index field is case sensitive, and entries must be written and spelled consistently. Otherwise, all the different ways you write or spell an entry will show up in the index.*

4. Sort the list (alphabetize) when you're finished (see page 91 for instructions on sorting lists) to make matching it up with the document easier.

Marking Main Entries

Marking entries one at a time gives you the opportunity to decide at every occurrence of a word or phrase whether or not it should be included in the index. To view nonprinting characters, click the Show/Hide button.

1. From the top of the document to be indexed, press Ctrl+F to find the text to mark (see how on page 14).

2. If this occurrence of the text is what you want in your index, select it. If not, click Find Next until you find the appropriate text.

3. With the text selected, press Alt+Shift+X to bring up the Mark Index Entry dialog box. The text you selected is already listed in the Main entry box.

4. If you have no subentry for this text, click Mark to mark just that one occurrence, or click Mark All to mark all occurrences of the word or phrase.

Note: Mark All will mark every occurrence of the word or phrase, whether it's appropriate for the index or not. In most cases, you will fare better marking the text one occurrence at a time.

5. If you have a subentry for this text, refer to the next section on marking subentries.

Note: If at any time the dialog box blocks your view, click the blue Title Bar on the dialog box, and drag it out of your way.

Marking Subentries

To create subentries in the document you want indexed:

1. Find the text you want as the subentry, and click the space immediately behind it.

2. Press Alt+Shift+X to bring up the Mark Index Entry dialog box/type the text for the Main entry box. Then type the Subentry in the Subentry box/click Mark or Mark All.

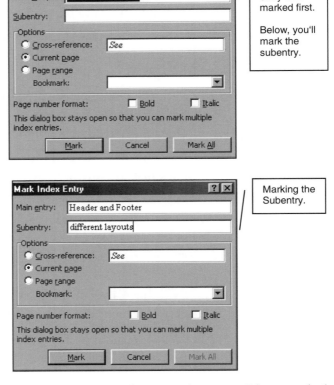

3. Repeat these steps for several entries. It's a good idea to create the index after you mark a few entries to see if you're doing it correctly. You'll be able to update, change, or delete entries later.

Creating the Index

Once your words and/or phrases are marked, you can create the index. Word will find all the index fields in your document and create the index.

From inside the document you want to index, **turn off the Show/Hide button** (leaving the nonprinting characters displayed will throw off your page numbering).

1. Create a blank page in back of your document for your index (insert a Section Break if you want to number the index pages differently from your document pages). Type the title, Index or something similar, and space down twice. You can format the title later.

2. Click Insert/Index and Tables/click the Index tab/choose desired format/click OK.

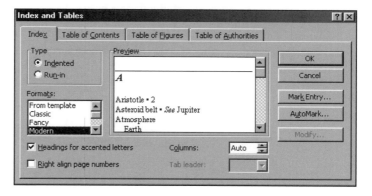

3. Once the Index is created, you'll see very clearly how you're doing with marking text. (Now you'll see why I mentioned that trial and error thing earlier.)

4. Make any adjustments necessary, either through deleting the entry and remarking the text, or manually changing how the index field reads (see how on page 40).

Reading the Index Field

With the Show/Hide button activated, you can actually see the index fields in your document. These are examples of how to read them.

- Different Layout of Headers and Footers{ XE "Header and Footer:different layouts" }¤

Colon

The index field starts with { XE.

Header and Footer: shows that Header and Footer was the Main Index entry.

The colon says that the Subentry, different layouts, will be listed under Header and Footer in the index.

"Symbols{ XE "symbols" }{ XE "symbols" \t "See also international characters and graphical typefaces" }¤

The first entry shows an index entry for "symbols." It will be listed in the index under "S" and in lower case.

Then another entry was marked as a cross-reference to "See also international characters and graphical typefaces."

A cross-reference is preceded by \t.

"Header and Footer{ XE "Header and Footer" \r "HeaderFooter" }¤

This is how an entry looks when a Bookmark has been applied.

In this case, a Bookmark named HeaderFooter had been created and was marked in the document next to the Header and Footer topic heading.

A Bookmark name is preceded by \r.

Cross-References as Index Entries

At times, you may want to refer the reader to other index entries. You can create an index entry as a cross-reference.

Inside your marked document, display nonprinting characters by clicking the Show/Hide toolbar button.

1. Mark the entry as you normally would so the page number it appears on will display in the index. (If you're simply referring the reader to another entry, you won't need to do this step.)

2. Click behind the field code of the entry that you want to create a cross-reference for, and press Alt+Shift+X to display the Mark Index Entry dialog box.

3. Type your Main entry (and Subentry if needed), and complete the information under Cross-reference.

4. Click Mark/repeat for each entry or Close.

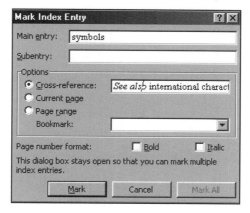

This is how the index entry will look:

> symbols, page no. *See also* international characters and graphical typefaces.

Deleting an Index Entry

You may later decide that some instances of a word or phrase do not need to be listed in the index. To delete the index entry:

1. Click the Show/Hide button to view nonprinting characters.

2. Click behind the index field that you want to delete/press Backspace once to highlight the field/press the Delete key/repeat steps as needed.

Changing an Index Entry

To change an entry, you can either delete it and remark the text, or you can change it manually.

1. Click the Show/Hide button to view nonprinting characters.

2. Change only the main and/or subentry text as you would normally edit text.

Note: To change the formatting of the text as it appears in your index, you have to edit the Index Styles (see Styles beginning on page 65). You can access the Style dialog box while in the Insert/Index and Tables dialog box by clicking Modify.

Updating the Index

Whenever you make changes to the document, you can quickly update your index without printing the document.

1. **Turn off the Show/Hide button** (leaving it activated will throw off your page numbering).

2. Go to any page in your index, and right-click on any paragraph.

3. Click Update Field.

Deleting the Index

1. Go to the beginning of the Index, and right-click anywhere on the Index/click Toggle Field Codes/select the Index field code/press Delete.

Creating Bookmark Entries

As mentioned earlier, it's a good idea to have your Bookmarks already created in your document. Using Bookmarks, you can create page ranges and reference them in your index.

When all the information related to a topic spans over several pages in your document, the first mention of it in the index should display this page range.

1. Click the Show/Hide button to display nonprinting characters.

2. Assuming you have already created Bookmarks throughout your document, find the occurrence of the word or phrase you want.

3. Select the text you want to mark, or click behind it or behind the last index field already listed. Then, press Alt+Shift+X to display the Mark Index Entry dialog box.

4. The text you selected is already in the Main entry box (otherwise, type it), so click the Page range Bookmark drop-down arrow, and choose the appropriate Bookmark name.

5. Click Mark/repeat for the next entry or Close.

This is how an index entry will look:

Header and Footer, page range.

Concordance File

The table you created earlier in this section is called a *concordance* file. You can point to this table from the Insert/Index and Tables dialog box, and let Word mark everything in the table at one time.

However, Word will mark *every* occurrence (including the TOC), whether it should be in the index or not. You can then delete unwanted entries as necessary.

This feature works great if you're creating a document with a lot of uncommon terms. You could use the concordance file to mark all of the uncommon terms at once. Then you could mark all the common terms one at a time as described earlier.

1. Follow the instructions for creating an index as explained on page 37. But, instead of clicking OK to create the index, click AutoMark/browse to find the concordance file you saved, and double-click it.

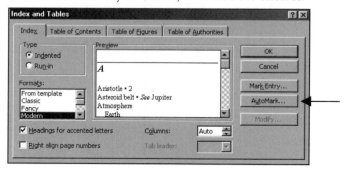

2. Word marks *every* occurrence of the word or phrase you indicated in the first column of your concordance file.

3. Word then uses the text in the second column as the actual index entry text. It will recognize the colon as a subentry.

Hyperlinks

To insert a link to other documents, particular sections of a document, or to a Web site, create a hyperlink.

1. Click Insert/Hyperlink (or click the toolbar button). (See more steps in the diagram.)

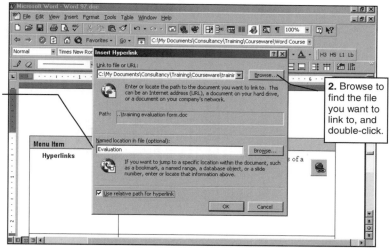

3. To have the link go to a certain section of this document or any document, direct the link to a Bookmark.

4. Click OK.

2. Browse to find the file you want to link to, and double-click.

Change or Edit the Hyperlink

You may want to change how your hyperlink reads.

1. Back in your document, right-click the hyperlink/point to Hyperlink/click Select Hyperlink.

2. While the Hyperlink is selected, retype its description.

If you want to edit the Hyperlink (change the link):

1. Right-click on the hyperlink in your document/point to Hyperlink/click Edit Hyperlink/make changes.

Note: *If you don't want Word to automatically change any URL you type into a hyperlink, click Tools/AutoCorrect/click the Autoformat As You Type tab/uncheck Internet and network paths with hyperlinks/click OK.*

Symbols

You can insert special characters, international characters, and symbols into your document.

1. Click Insert/Symbol.

2. Change the font to see which symbols come with each.

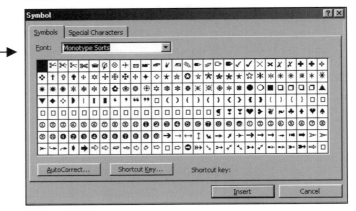

3. Double-click the symbol you want to insert into your document/click Close.

While you're in this box, click on the Special Characters tab and see what's in store.

If there is a symbol you use often, you can create it as a keyboard shortcut.

1. Click Insert/Symbol/select the symbol you want/click Shortcut Key/press the desired shortcut keys/click Add/Close/Close. (*Refer to section on creating Macros as a Keyboard Shortcut on page 84 for more information.*)

Note: See the back of the Word section for samples of symbols or graphical typefaces.

Cross-References

Throughout this book, you've been advised to refer to another page for more information on a particular topic. These are called "cross-references" and are easy to create in Word. In this case, the page number of a particular heading will be cross-referenced. The cross-reference was prefaced with, "For more information on ..., see page ".

To create the cross-reference, type your preface statement and space over once:

1. Click Insert/Cross-reference/choose the Reference type (which in this case is Heading).

2. Choose the Insert reference to (which in this case is the Page number).

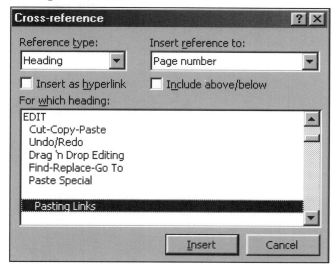

3. Click the desired Heading/click Insert/Close.

In this case, the page number that the heading, "Pasting Links," is on will appear in your document as a field, and will be automatically updated if the page number ever changes.

AutoText

Use AutoText to store your company logo, a complicated formula, sentences you use often, paragraphs you need on occasion, etc. Once it's saved as an AutoText entry, you can insert it anywhere you want it the instant you need it. The first thing you have to do is create the entry. You might want your company logo as an AutoText entry:

1. Display your logo on a page, and select it.
2. While the logo is selected, click Insert/point to AutoText/click New.
3. Give the AutoText entry a name (i.e., mylogo).
4. Now, every time you need your company logo to appear in a document, all you have to do is type the name you gave the AutoText entry (mylogo), and press F3.

If you forget the name of your entry:

1. Click Insert/AutoText/AutoText.

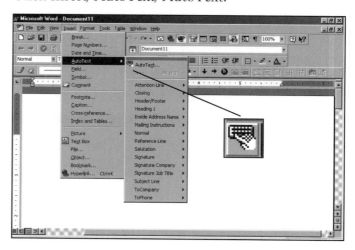

There are other AutoText options on the Header/Footer toolbar (see Header/Footer information on page 18).

Footnotes / Endnotes

1. Click behind text where you want the footnote or endnote indicated/click Insert/Footnote/choose desired options/OK/type text for footnote/click in document to resume editing.

    Note: *You can also create a cross-reference to a previously mentioned footnote (see Cross-References on page 45).*

Organization Charts

1. Click Insert/Object/click Create New tab/scroll to find the MS Organization Chart /double-click it. You're now working inside the MS Org Chart software. Word is in the background.

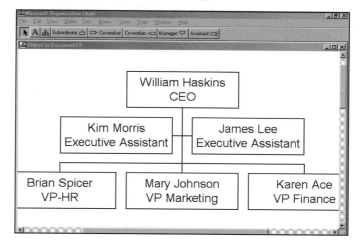

To create this chart from inside MS Organization Chart:

1. Select the default title, and type chart title.

2. Click inside top box, and type the CEO's name, tab to type the title, CEO, then click outside the box so information will be entered.

3. The CEO has **two** assistants, so click the Assistant toolbar button **twice**, then click the CEO's box once. Type information into the new boxes.

4. If Brian had three people reporting to him, you

would click the Subordinate toolbar button three times, then click his box once to create three boxes.

5. If the CEO hired another VP, he/she would be entered into the chart as a co-worker of Brian, Mary, and Karen.

6. Select boxes if you want to delete one or change box styles and line colors with the toolbar buttons.

7. Click File/Close to return to your Word document.

8. To make changes later, double-click the chart from Word to get back to MS Organizational Chart.

Tips for MS Organizational Charts

- To display drawing tools, click View/Show Draw Tools.

- To change text color, box style, background color, etc., refer to the appropriate menu items.

- Press Ctrl+A to select all boxes.

- To deselect a box, hold the Shift key down, and click the box you don't want selected.

- To select all the boxes in a group, double-click one of the boxes in the group. Example: To select all Vice Presidents in this chart, double-click Brian's box.

- To move the entire chart either up or down on the page, drag the topmost box up or down.

- To select an entire branch of the chart, select the topmost box in the branch, and press Ctrl+B.

- To convert a box from one type to another, drag the box so it attaches to the type of box you want it to be.

- To delete a box, select it, and press the Delete key.

FORMAT

Format Font

1. Select the text you want to change/press Ctrl+D (**Or,** click Format/Font).

   You can make these changes your default by clicking Default on the Format Font dialog box (bottom left-hand corner), thereby saving the changes as part of Word's default template, normal. (*See page 10 for more information.*)

Resizing Text

A shortcut to resizing your text:

1. Select the text/press Ctrl+] to make it larger, or press Ctrl+[to make it smaller.

Format Font Toolbar Buttons

You can also change the font name, style, size, and alignment from the Formatting toolbar.

1. Select text/click appropriate toolbar button to change. Re-click the B, I, or U buttons to turn off.

Change Case

You can quickly change capitalizations.

1. Select the text/press Shift+F3 until the text is the case you want (**or,** click Format/Change Case). If you need to select the entire document, press Ctrl+A.

Text Direction

1. Select the text you want to change.

2. Click the Text Direction toolbar button until your text is displayed the way you want it. This toolbar button is located on the Drawing Toolbar. (*Refer to page 22 for help on displaying toolbars.*)

Paragraph Mark

Formatting for the paragraph is collected in the paragraph end mark. That's why when you press Enter to create another paragraph, the formatting comes with it.

You'll have to activate your Show/Hide toolbar button to be able to see this nonprinting character. ¶

Format Paragraph

1. Click Format/Paragraph to change line spacing, breaks, indentation, and alignment.

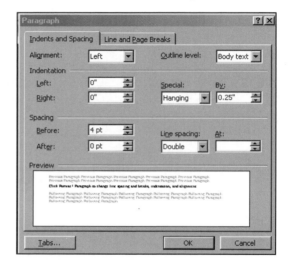

Paragraph Spacing

Set spacing to automatically put a designated amount of space before or after each paragraph every time you press Enter.

1. Select the paragraph you want to adjust/click Format/Paragraph/adjust Spacing Before or After.

Note: *You can change the line spacing in this dialog box, or as explained on the following page.*

WORD

Line Spacing

Select the text to be changed, then press:

- ▤ Ctrl+1 = single space
- ▤ Ctrl+5 = 1.5 space
- ▤ Ctrl+2 = double space
- ▤ Ctrl+0 = add 12 points of space before the paragraph.
- ▤ Ctrl+Shift+0 = remove space before the paragraph.

Line Break

To create a new line without creating a new paragraph:

1. Press Shift+Enter.

Drop Cap

1. Click in front of the first letter of the sentence where you want a drop cap to appear.

2. Click Format/Drop Cap/choose the Position and Options you want/click OK.

Format Painter

The Format Painter can be used to *brush* the format of one paragraph or word onto another.

Example: You've just made a paragraph bright blue, indented it, and changed the typeface so it's different from the rest of your document.

You want to apply this same formatting to two other paragraphs in your document.

1. Click your Show/Hide button so you can see the Paragraph Mark at the end of the paragraph (see page 50 for information on the paragraph mark).
2. Select the Paragraph Mark.
3. Double-click the Format Painter toolbar button (double-clicking the Painter lets you use it more than once).
4. Brush the painter over the other two paragraphs you want to format.
5. Press Esc when finished.

If you want to paint the formatting of a word onto other text, just select the formatted word, then follow steps 3-5 above.

To remove the formatting and return the text to its original state:

1. Select the text/press Ctrl+Shift+N.

AutoFormat

Word can format your document automatically by adding bullets, numbering, heading styles, etc.

1. Type your document without any special formatting, using an * to indicate a bulleted list item.

2. Click Format/AutoFormat.

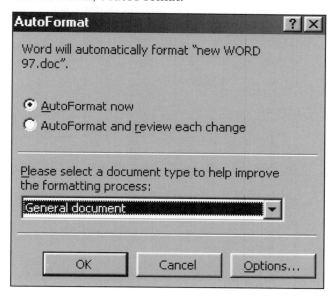

3. Choose to either AutoFormat now or AutoFormat and review each change.

4. Select desired document type/change Options if needed/click OK.

If you have a document that has been converted from another format and it has hard returns at the end of each line, you can remove them easily.

1. Follow steps 2-4 above, but when you click Options, uncheck all the boxes.

Borders

Borders can be added around a paragraph, a page, or a cell in a table. To create a bordered paragraph:

1. Select the paragraph(s) to be changed.

2. Click Format/Borders and Shading/Borders tab.

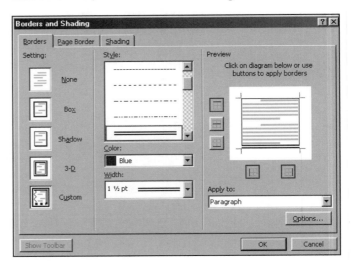

In this case, the Box Setting was clicked to put a box around the paragraph. The bottom border of the paragraph needed to be a double blue line.

3. Click Custom Setting.

4. Click scroll bar on the line Style box to find a double line/click the desired line style.

5. Change Line Color to Blue.

6. Change line width to 1 ½ pt.

7. Click the bottom border of the box in the far-right Preview box/OK. If you need to adjust the internal margins of the border, click Options before OK.

Shading

Shading can be added to a paragraph to make certain sections stand out.

1. Select the paragraph(s) to be changed.
2. Click Format/Borders and Shading/Shading tab/make your choices as described below.

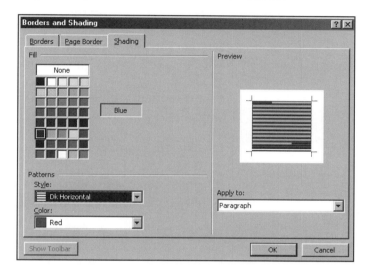

- ▣ **Fill** is the color you want for shading. Choose None for no color.
- ▣ **Pattern** is the shading style and color you want to lay on top of the fill color. **Clear** will apply only the fill color and no pattern color. **Solid** will apply only the pattern color and no fill color. **Color** is for the lines and dots of the pattern style.

In this case, the Fill color blue was selected; horizontal lines will lay on top of the blue Fill color; and the horizontal lines will be red. If printing to a black and white printer, choose Auto or Black as the color.

Tabs

One of the worst things you can do in your document is to try to use the spacebar to align data (it will not work), or tab more than once to get to your next tab stop.

If you don't take the time to set up your tab stops, you end up spending too much time creating and revising your document. Tabbing three or four times to get to the next column is a waste, and when you try to revise the data later, you'll see it scatter all over the page. This then will cause you to waste more time trying to fix it.

Take a moment up front to set your tab stops (or create a table). This will save you so much time in the end.

1. Click in your document where you want tabs to begin/click Format/Tabs/type the desired tab stop position/choose alignment for that tab stop/click Set. Repeat for each tab position.

To return the document to the default settings:

1. Click where you want to restart default tab settings/click Format/Tabs/click Clear All/OK.

Note: If you decide to change the tab stops later, select the tabbed text before you click Format/Tabs and change.

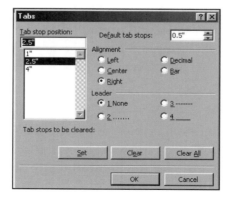

Changing Tabs Using the Horizontal Ruler

For a quicker way to set your tab stops, try this:

1. Click once in your document where you want to create the tab stops.

2. Move the mouse pointer to the horizontal ruler, and click where tab stops should be.

    Tab markers will indicate where tab stops are and the type of tab you set. You can change all this later.

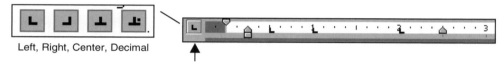

Left, Right, Center, Decimal

To vary the types of tab you set:

1. Click the button at the left-end of the ruler until you see the type of tab you want.

2. Click the horizontal ruler at the desired tab stops.

Note: If you're going to change tab stops for text you've already typed, you have to select the text first, then change the tab stops.

To change the tab position:

1. Click on a tab marker, and drag it to its new location.

To remove a tab position:

1. Click on the tab marker, and drag it off the ruler.

To return to the default tab settings after you've finished typing the tabbed text:

1. Click where you want tab settings to stop/drag the tab markers off the ruler/type the remaining of your text.

Margins and Indents

Change the margin indent only when you're changing the margin for the entire document or for a very large section. Otherwise, change the indents with the Increase or Decrease Indent toolbar buttons as described in "Adding Subordinate Paragraphs" on page 59.

1. Click the horizontal ruler, and drag markers as desired.

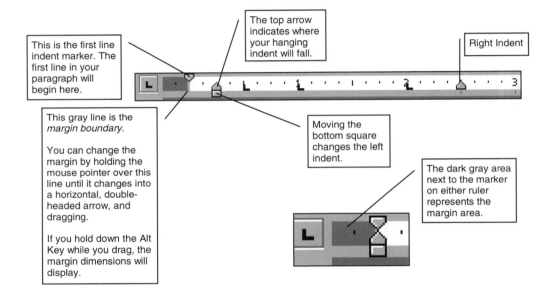

The top arrow indicates where your hanging indent will fall.

Right Indent

This is the first line indent marker. The first line in your paragraph will begin here.

This gray line is the *margin boundary*.

You can change the margin by holding the mouse pointer over this line until it changes into a horizontal, double-headed arrow, and dragging.

If you hold down the Alt Key while you drag, the margin dimensions will display.

Moving the bottom square changes the left indent.

The dark gray area next to the marker on either ruler represents the margin area.

Numbered Lists

You can number paragraphs to depict steps or a series. A quick way to create a numbered list is as follows:

1. Type 1. and press Tab/type your text/press Enter to create the second numbered paragraph. Automatic numbering will begin.

2. End the numbered paragraphs by pressing Enter twice.

The following information gets into more detail about creating and reformatting numbered lists.

Numbering Toolbar Button

Another way to create a numbered list is by using the Numbering toolbar button.

1. Click the Numbering toolbar button to turn numbers on, and start your list (or create the list first, select it, and click the button).

2. Click the button again to turn numbering off.

Adding Subordinate Paragraphs

To turn numbering off in the middle of a list:

1. Click in front of the numbered paragraph in which you don't want numbering.

2. Click the Numbering toolbar button to turn it off.

3. Click the Increase Indent button on the Formatting toolbar to line the text up properly (or press Ctrl+M to increase indent, and Ctrl+Shift+M to decrease).

Restart Numbering

When you have several numbered lists throughout your document, and the numbering has continued from the previous list, you can change the numbering to restart at "1."

Example: When your numbered paragraph starts at 5 and you want it to start over at 1:

1. Click in the paragraph where you want the numbering to restart at 1/click Format/Bullets and Numbering/click the Numbered tab/choose to Restart numbering.

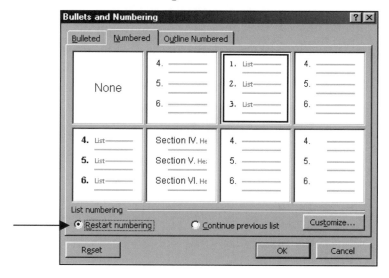

Note: *This mundane step is perfect for a macro. You'll learn why and how when you explore this timesaving feature on page 81.*

Changing
Number
Format

You can change the formatting of your numbers:

1. Select the numbered text/click Format/Bullets and Numbering.

2. On the Numbered tab, click the desired number format.

Numbered lists can be customized to include text before or after the number. For example, to include the word "Series" before the number in a list:

1. Click Format/Bullets and Numbering.

2. On the Numbered tab, click the desired number format/click Customize.

3. Click in front of the number in the Number Format box/type the word "Series"/space once/make any other desired changes/click OK.

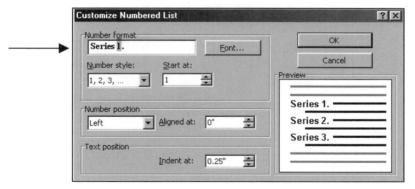

Inside this box, you can also change the font, the number style, the starting number, and the number and text position.

Outline Numbered Lists

You can easily create numbering for an outline or legal document by using Word's Outline Numbering feature.

1. Click Format/Bullets and Numbering.

2. Click the Outline Numbered tab/click the desired number format/click Customize.

3. Click on the first level, and customize it.

4. Repeat for subsequent levels one at the time.

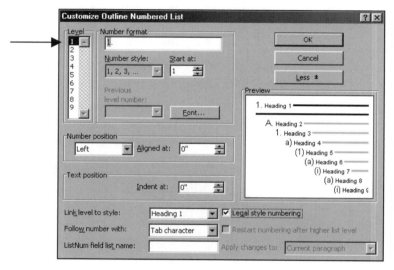

5. To view more options, click More (this button changes to Less, depending on which view you're in).

Back in your document, follow the instructions on the screen below to type your list for the outline.

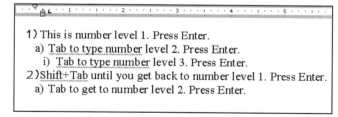

Bulleted Lists

Bulleted lists work basically the same as numbered lists as explained beginning on page 59.

To change the look of the default bullets:

1. Select the bulleted text/click Format/Bullets and Numbering/Customize/Bullet.

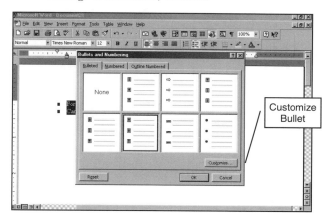

If you prefer still another type of bullet:

1. Click the Customize button.

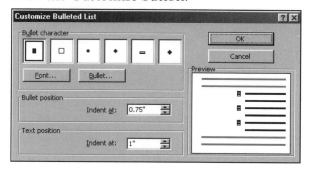

2. Click Font to change the font formatting, or click Bullet to change the style of the bullet.

Note: *To quickly start a bulleted list, type an */press tab/type your text/press Enter to go to the next line.*

Columns (Newspaper)

Newspaper columns flow from the bottom of one column to the next.

1. Click Format/Columns/click one of the Presets buttons/click Line between if needed/OK.

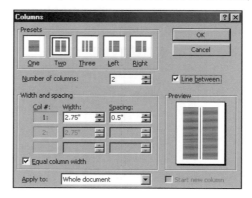

Note: See the section on Linked Text Boxes on page 25 for another way to create newsletters.

Sections

If you want different numbers or styles of columns on the same page, you'll have to divide your document into continuous Sections. Sections in a document can be formatted independently. (See on-screen instructions.)

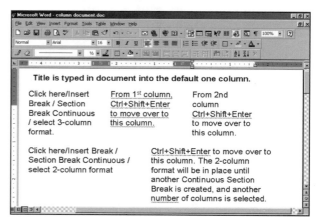

Styles

A style is a set of formatting instructions saved with a style name. Applying a style to text will format it consistently every time.

Once a style is applied to the text, changing it is easy. Simply change the attributes of the style applied to it. All the text with that style applied to it will reformat to match the new formatting.

You'll need to understand Heading Levels as explained on page 28 to grasp the concept of Styles.

Applying Styles from the Toolbar

Word has several built-in styles. To apply one to a paragraph from the Formatting toolbar:

1. Click inside the paragraph you want to apply the style to.

2. Click the Style List box drop-down arrow/click the desired style.

Style List Box

Note: *To see every available style in Word, hold down the Shift key before you click the drop-down arrow in the Style List box.*

Applying Styles from the Menu

To apply a style from the Menu Bar:

1. Select the paragraph you want to apply the style to.

2. Click Format/Style/click desired style/Apply.

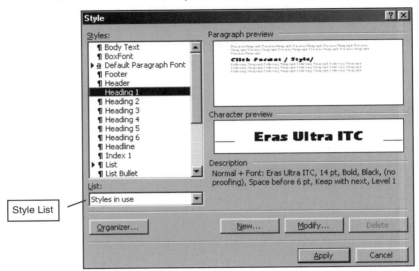

In the Style List, you can display:

- **Styles in Use.** Lists standard styles and styles you have created or changed for the current document.

- **All Styles.** Lists all styles available in Word.

- **User-Defined Styles.** Lists only styles you have created for the current document.

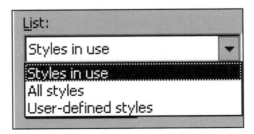

Redefining Style Attributes

To change style attributes of a style already applied:

1. Select the paragraph you want to change the style of.

2. Increase the font size, change the typeface, add a border, or make whatever other changes you want.

3. Click the down arrow next to the Style List box, and click the name of the style you just changed.

4. Click Update the style to reflect recent changes/OK. The style will be reformatted, and all the text with that style applied to it will change also.

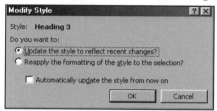

Changing Style Attributes from the Menu

1. Select the paragraph you want to change the style of.

2. Click Format/Style/select the Style you want to change (if not already selected).

3. Click Modify/Format/choose the attribute you want to change, and make the changes.

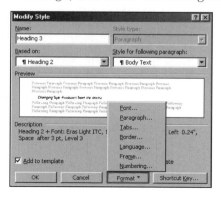

4. Click Add to Template/OK/Close.

Creating a Style

You can also create your own styles. However, to make creating your Table of Contents easier, keep the names of your *main heading levels* the same as Word has them. You can change the attributes, but keep the name as it is.

1. Click Format/Style/New.

2. Name the new style.

3. In the Based on box, click the name of a style that is the most like the new one.

4. In the Style for the following paragraph box, select which style will probably follow the new style when you press Enter.

5. Change any formatting as you normally would.

6. Click Add to Template/OK.

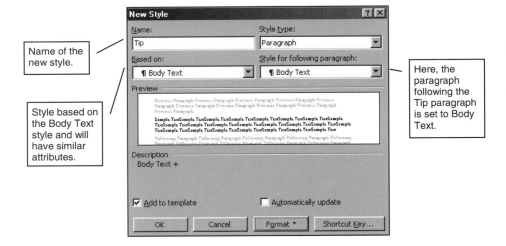

Name of the new style.

Style based on the Body Text style and will have similar attributes.

Here, the paragraph following the Tip paragraph is set to Body Text.

TOOLS

Tools/Options

The default instructions on how Word handles your work might not be what you want. **Always** set your software to run with your preferences.

1. Click Tools/Options to see what you want to change.

AutoCorrect

As you are typing in your document, you sometimes make common typing and spelling errors. Word's AutoCorrect feature automatically corrects these errors. This feature will also let you replace a word or symbol with a graphic. AutoCorrect has rules that say, "when you do this, Word will do this." You can use Word's built-in rules, and you can also make up your own. You can also turn rules off.

1. Click Tools/AutoCorrect/review choices on the AutoCorrect tab.

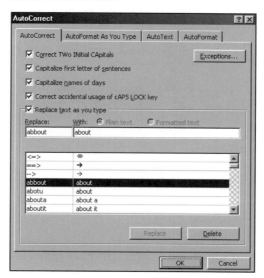

Note: Use AutoCorrect to help you type international names quickly. See Typing International Characters on page 98.

Exception   You can instruct Word as to when to make an exception to your rule.

Example: Suppose you turned on the rule to correct two initial caps typed together. But, your company's name should be written SIms, and every time you type it, Word changes it to read Sims.

You can create an exception that tells Word to leave your company name with the first two initial caps.

1. Click Tools/AutoCorrect/Exceptions/create the entry not to be corrected/click Add/OK.

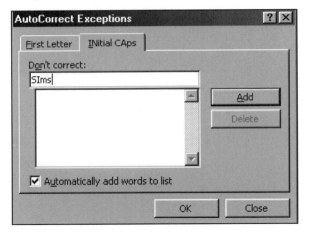

To have Word automatically add entries to the list, make sure the "Automatically add words to list" check box is checked on the AutoCorrect Exceptions dialog box.

Then, in your document, if you type the word and Word changes it, you can **backspace** to fix the word. Word will automatically put the word in your Exceptions list. This will not work if you clicked Undo in an attempt to correct the word.

Adding a Rule

If you want to add other words you commonly mistype:

1. Continuing from the AutoCorrect tab, click inside the Replace box on the AutoCorrect tab/type the word the way you do when you mistype it.

2. Click inside the Replace with box, and type the correct spelling in the With box/click Add/OK.

Note*: To have a rule that replaces something with a graphic (i.e., your logo), select the graphic before clicking Tools/AutoCorrect.*

Auto Complete

Sample Tip

AutoComplete lets you insert items such as dates and AutoText entries when you type a few identifying characters. Press Enter when the tip displays if you want to insert the item into your document.

To turn off the AutoComplete tips or to view, delete, or insert AutoText entries:

1. Click Tools/AutoCorrect/AutoText tab.

**AutoFormat
As You Type**
Also a part of the AutoCorrect dialog box is this feature that automatically formats headings, bulleted and numbered lists, borders, numbers, symbols, etc., as you type.

1. Click the AutoFormat As You Type tab/click desired options/OK.

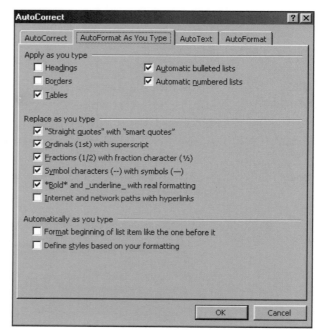

Note: *To automatically format selected text (or an entire document you have received) based on the Options you have selected here, use the Format/AutoFormat command. See page 53 for more information on AutoFormat.*

Auto Summarize

If you receive a lengthy document and are only interested in the key points, Word can summarize the document for you.

1. Click Tools/AutoSummarize/click your choices/OK.

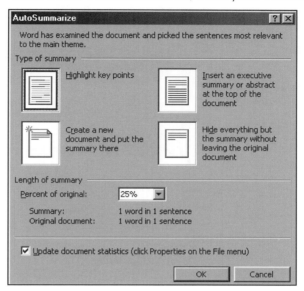

Dictionary-Customizing

You can create a custom dictionary and add words you use often. It's a good idea to add terms specific to your industry or company.

1. From inside a blank document, click Tools/Options/Spelling & Grammar tab/Dictionaries.

2. Select the Custom Dictionary if not checked.

3. Click Edit/add desired words in a single column, pressing Enter at the end of each line/click Save.

Spelling Check

If you have Check Spelling as You Type turned on in Tools/Options/Spelling, Word underlines misspelled words with a wavy, red line. To run the Spelling Checker:

1. Click Tools/Spelling and Grammar (or click the toolbar button). Here, the Spelling Checker noted that the word "documant" is misspelled.

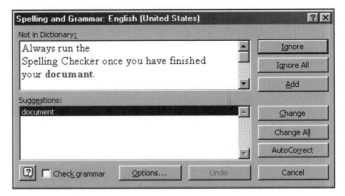

2. Check the Suggestions box for possible spelling choices, and double-click the correctly spelled version.

3. If you don't see the correct spelling in the Suggestions box, double-click the misspelled word in the Not in Dictionary text box/type the correct spelling/click Change or Change All.

4. For a word that is not really misspelled, but a special term you use, click Ignore or Ignore All.

5. If a highlighted word is not a misspelling, but in fact a word you need to add to the dictionary, click Add.

6. To have an AutoCorrect entry created that will always change this particular error to the correct spelling as you type, click AutoCorrect.

Note: To only check the spelling of the word that has the wavy, red line under it, right-click on it.

Envelopes

1. Click Tools/Envelopes and Labels/click the Envelopes tab.

2. Type the delivery address.

3. If you're using pre-printed envelopes, click to Omit the Return address.

4. Click the Feed box if you need to alter the way the envelope will feed into the printer.

5. Click the Options button to make additional changes such as having a bar code print.

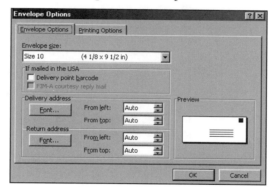

6. Click Add to Document if you want the envelope to be added to your document. Otherwise, put the envelope in your printer, and click Print.

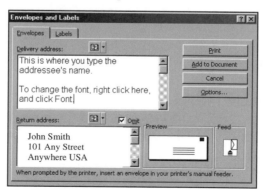

Labels

Word comes will all types of label formats for pre-packaged labels. If you need to create labels:

1. Click Tools/Envelopes and Labels/click Labels tab.

2. If you need to use a different type of label other than the one already listed, click Options.

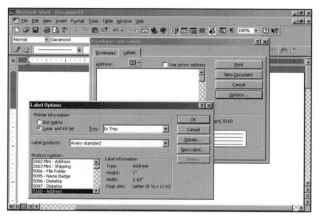

3. Find the type of label that matches the ones you'll put in your printer, and click it/click OK.

4. If you need to format the label sheet from inside your document, click New Document. Otherwise, decide if you want to print a full page with the same label or just one.

Print Full Page of Same Labels

If you're creating the same label for the entire sheet:

1. Continuing from above, type the information in the Address box/click Full page of the same label/put label sheet in the printer/click Print.

Note: Labels are created using Word tables. If an address splits across pages, refer to the section, "Change Cell Size" on page 90 to learn how to keep the table row from splitting.

Print One Label

If you're only creating one label:

1. Type the information in the Address box.

2. Click Single Label/click arrows to find the row and column that match the available labels on the sheet.

3. Put label sheet in the printer/click Print.

Mail Merge

You can quickly produce mass mailings to all or just some of the people in your database of names and addresses. Your database can be an Excel spreadsheet, Word table, Access table, or Contact list as in Outlook, etc., or some similar program.

For mail merge to work, you must set up a database of records with fields.

The best example of a database is the phone directory. All the information about you in the phone directory makes up your *record*, including your name, address, city, etc. Each one of these items in your record is called a *field*.

Courtesy Title	Last	First	Generation	Title

This entire row of information is a record.

Merging

In the following example, form letters will be created. Using the advantages of Mail Merge, you can also create mailing envelopes, labels, catalogs, or forms.

1. From an open document, click Tools/Mail Merge.

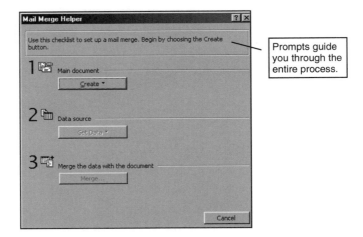

2. Click Create/Form letters/Active Window (which just says you'll create the mail merge document in the open Word document).

Note: If you need mailing labels, refer to page 76 to understand how labels are created before you mail merge.

The next step is to tell Word where your database of names and addresses (your contacts list) is:

3. Click Get Data, and make your selection to Open Data Source or Use Address Book (or Create one if you don't have one) /click Edit Main Document.

Note: If you use Outlook for your contacts list, you'll choose Use Address Book in this step.

The Mail Merge toolbar will now be displayed inside your Main Document.

From the Mail Merge toolbar, you will place the desired fields into your document.

4. Click on your document page where you want the text to appear/click the Insert Merge Field drop-down arrow, and click the appropriate merge field needed in your document. Place each field as you need them to print (i.e., if information in your document requires a space between them (as in City State Zip), you should place spaces between each merge field.

5. Repeat step 4 until you have finished placing all of the fields in your document.

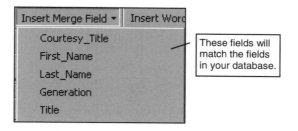

These fields will match the fields in your database.

The next step is to Merge.

6. Decide whether to mail merge to a New Document, Printer, or to change Merge Options.

Merge Options

**Query
Options**

To filter the database so you can address information to a certain group, or only to people in a certain city, etc., a Query will have to be performed.

1. Click the Mail Merge Options button.

2. Click Query Options.

The instructions below describe how letters can be sent to Atlanta CEOs only.

3. Click the drop-down arrow next to the Field box, and choose "City."

4. Click the drop-down arrow under Comparison, and choose Equal to/type Atlanta in the Compare to box.

5. Change the Title field to Equal to CEO.

6. Click the Sort Records tab if you need to sort the list/click OK/Merge.

Remove a Data Source

If you need to remove a data source from a document (the file with the names and addresses that you used during the mail merge needs to be detached):

1. Open the document/click Tools/Mail Merge/Create/Restore to Normal Word Document/click OK.

Macros

A macro is the recording of a sequence of mouse clicks and keystrokes that can be played back whenever you need it. You can build the macro as a keyboard shortcut or create your own toolbar button.

As Toolbar Button

1. Click Tools/Macro/Record New Macro.
2. Give the macro a name (can't use spaces, punctuation marks, or other similar characters). The name can contain up to 40 characters.
3. Choose where to store the macro (i.e., either make it available to all documents or only to the one you are working in).
4. Type a description of the macro.
5. Click the Toolbars button so you can create your own button. When you're finished, you'll be able to click your new toolbar button to start the macro.

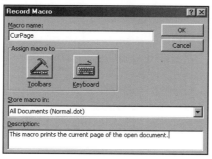

Customize Toolbar Button

The screen below depicts how you can customize your toolbar button.

1. Click on the new Command, and drag it to the toolbar and drop it.

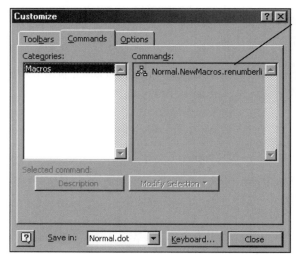

Click inside Command box and drag the icon to the toolbar and drop it.

2. The elongated I-beam will indicate where the toolbar button will go when the mouse is released.

    ▤ While in this dialog box, you can remove a toolbar button by clicking on the toolbar, and dragging it off.

    ▤ If you're not in this dialog box, and you want to remove a toolbar button, hold down Alt, and drag the button off the toolbar.

3. You'll now need to modify the button while you're still in the Customize Macro dialog box.

WORD

Modify Toolbar Button

While you're in the Customize Macro dialog box, you can change the face of your toolbar button.

1. Right-click on the new button.

2. Click Text only (in Menus) because in this case, you don't want text on your button—text will only be in the Menus.

3. Right-click on the new button again (or click Modify Selection) /point to Change Button Image, and choose an icon.

Note: *If you want text on your button, leave the Text Only (Always) selection checked, and click in the Name box to type new name.*

4. Click Close. The Macro Recorder now records what you do. (You'll notice a mini cassette that indicates recording.)

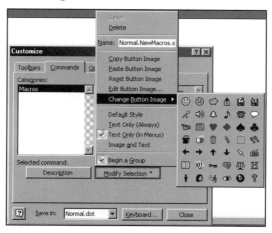

In this example, you'll record a macro that prints the current page you're working on.

5. Click File/Print/Current page/OK/stop the recording (click the square on the Record toolbar).

As Keyboard Shortcut

You can also build your macro and activate it with a keyboard shortcut.

1. Click Tools/Macro/Record New Macro.

2. Give the macro a name (can't use spaces, punctuation marks, or other similar characters. Name can contain up to 40 characters).

3. Type a description of the macro/click Keyboard.

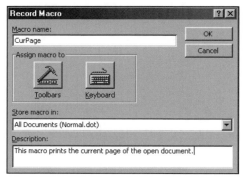

4. Now you have to assign the keyboard shortcut.

5. Click inside this box, and press the keyboard keys you want to assign the macro to. (Usually Alt+something will be available.)

Alt+B was available (unassigned).

6. Click Assign / Close / Record your macro.

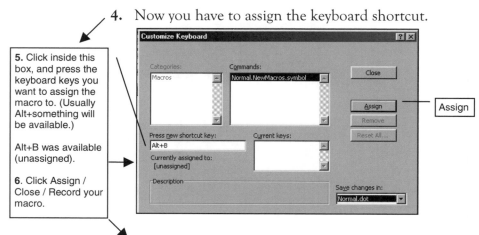

Assign

The Macro Recorder now records what you do.

7. Click File/Print/Current page/OK/stop recording.

Templates and Add-Ins

You can attach a template to an active document, and the active document will have the same styles, customized toolbars, macros, AutoText, and any keyboard shortcuts you created in the initial template.

From within the active document:

1. Click Tools/Templates and Add-Ins/Attach.

2. Browse to find the template you want to attach, and double-click the template name/click OK.

3. Click Automatically update document styles if you want Word to format the active document/click OK.

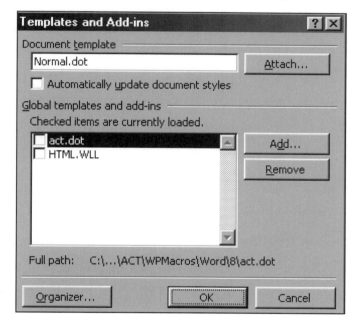

Organizer
Sometimes you may only want to transfer one or a few styles or AutoText entries from one template or document to another. This can be accomplished with the Organizer.

1. Open a document containing the attribute(s) you want to transfer.

2. Click Tools/Templates and Add-Ins/Organizer. The left side of the dialog box will show the active document. The right side will show the Normal template.

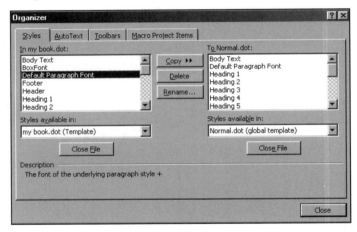

3. Click on the tab for the type of feature you want to transfer (Styles, AutoText, Toolbars, Macros).

Note: If you need to select a different document or template on either side, clicking the Close File button will change it into an Open File button. You can then browse to find the desired file.

4. Click the Styles tab/click on the style(s) in the left window, and Copy to the file in the right window.

5. Click Close when you're finished.

TABLE

Creating a Table

1. Click the Insert Table toolbar button. Click inside the table and drag out your rows and columns. You can add more later.

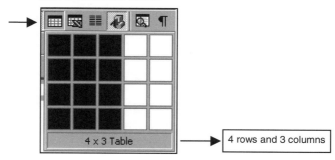

2. **Or,** click Table/Insert Table/type 3 for columns and 4 for rows/click OK.

Drawing a Table

You can draw the table with the software just as if you were sketching it with a pencil by using the Draw Table toolbar button.

1. Click the Draw Table tool, hold it over your document page/click and drag out your table, dragging across and down.

2. To correct an error, click the Erase tool, and drag over unwanted line(s).

3. Press Esc when finished.

Select Table

Click inside table. Click Alt+5 (from the numeric keypad). If Num Lock is down, click Shift+Alt+5.

Select a Cell

Point your mouse to the left of the cell until it turns into a solid, white arrow that turns toward the cell, and click.

Select a Row   Hold the mouse pointer to the left of the entire row (out into the left margin) until it turns into a solid, white arrow that turns toward the row, and click.

Select a Column   Hold the mouse pointer over the top of the column until the pointer turns into a thick, black arrow, and click.

Tab Inside Cell   Press Ctrl+Tab.

Typing Above Table

1. Click in the first cell in the table, and press Enter.
2. **Or,** click in the first cell in the table, and click Table/Split Table.

Headings On Each Page

If your table expands past one page, the column titles can be set to repeat on every page.

1. Select the row you want repeated on every page.
2. Click Table/Headings.

Convert Table To Text

1. Select table/click Table/Convert Table to Text (can also convert Text to Table if appropriate tab stops were used).

Aligning Text in Cells

You can quickly tell Word where you want your text to fall in the cell (top, middle, bottom) by clicking the corresponding toolbar button on the Tables and Borders toolbar (display the toolbar if not shown).

1. Select your cell(s)/click the desired toolbar button.

Merging / Splitting Cells

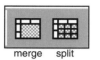

merge   split

You can create professional-looking forms by splitting and merging cells in a table.

1. Select the cells to be split or merged.
2. Click the appropriate toolbar button.

Inserting Rows and Columns

1. Select a row or column in the table.
2. Click Table/Insert Rows or Columns. Or click the Insert Row/Column toolbar button (the Table toolbar button changes from Insert/Table to Insert/Row or Column, depending on what you have selected).

   If you have selected a row and want to insert another one, the toolbar button changes to Insert Row. If you select two rows and click the Insert Row button, Word will insert two rows. The same applies to the column.

 Or

Note: *If you are in the very last cell of a table and want another row, press Tab.*

Numbering Items in a Table

1. Insert a blank column at the beginning of your table.
2. Select the new column/click the Numbering toolbar button.

Note: *You could also number the first column that has text.*

Insert Column at End of Table

If you need to insert a column at the end of your table:

1. Hold the mouse pointer over the space beside the last column (as if a column were actually there), and click after the mouse becomes a thick, black arrow). The blank space will be selected.

2. Click the Insert Column toolbar button.

Distribute Rows and Columns Evenly

You can also make all your rows or columns distribute evenly by selecting the rows or columns and clicking the appropriate toolbar button located on the Tables and Borders toolbar.

Change Cell Size

1. Click Table/Cell Height and Width/click Row tab.

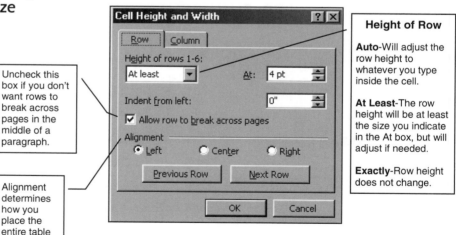

Uncheck this box if you don't want rows to break across pages in the middle of a paragraph.

Alignment determines how you place the entire table on the page.

Height of Row

Auto-Will adjust the row height to whatever you type inside the cell.

At Least-The row height will be at least the size you indicate in the At box, but will adjust if needed.

Exactly-Row height does not change.

2. Click the Column tab to make column adjustments.

**Shortcut to
Change
Table Cell
Size**

1. Select the row or column you want to resize, and hold the mouse directly over one of its borders.

2. When the mouse pointer turns into a double-headed arrow, drag the row or column to its new size. If text is already in the cell, double-click the border with the double-sided arrow to automatically adjust it.

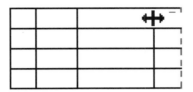

To resize a column without distorting the others, hold down the Shift key as you drag.

Sort

To sort the data in a table:

1. Select the column you want to sort by/click Table/Sort/make necessary changes/click OK.

Building Forms

A form can be any document that includes cells with or without fields that you can type into. Word's form features let you include text boxes, check boxes, radio buttons (options buttons), and drop-down boxes that contain ordered choices.

Once the form is created, it has to be Protected so users can enter information only into designated areas. In this example, a Book Order form was created as a template.

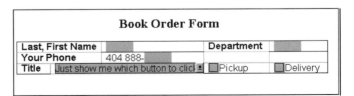

Create a table as you normally would (see page 87).

1. Display the Forms toolbar.

2. Click inside cell where a Name will be typed/click the Text Field button on the Forms toolbar. Repeat for the Department and Phone information.

3. Click inside the cell where the Book Title choices will be entered/click the Drop-Down Form Field button. Double-click the form field that's now inside the cell to add book titles.

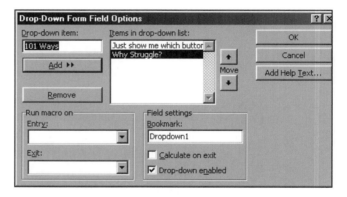

4. Type the first Drop-down item/click Add. Repeat for other items in the list/click OK. (Use the Move arrows to adjust the order.)

5. Back in your form, click in front of Pick Up/click the Check Box toolbar button. Repeat for Delivery.

6. Protect the form: click the Lock/Protect for Forms.

Note: Once the form is protected and data is entered into the form fields, if you unprotect the form, data typed in the fields is erased.

WINDOW

Click Window to switch between open documents within the same application (all open Word documents). (Press Alt+Tab to switch between all open applications.)

HELP

Help—What's This?

Help on a Word feature is a couple of mouse clicks away.

1. Click on the What's This? tool, hold it over a paragraph or toolbar button, etc., that you want to know about, and click.

    Note: *If you don't see the What's This? toolbar button, refer to the information on Customizing Toolbars on page 20 to display it.*

2. Press Esc to remove it.

You can also hold the What's This? tool over a paragraph and click to see what formatting is applied to the paragraph.

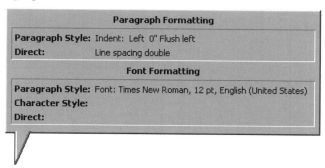

Help-How to Find It

To use Help to get assistance on a particular feature:

1. Click Help/Contents and Index/choose Index tab/type a subject/view choices/double-click your choice.

OTHER TOPICS

Hot Spots on Screen

Shortcuts to various computer commands include:

▤ Double-click anywhere on the ruler to go to Page Setup.

▤ Double-click on the grayed out REC button on the Status Bar to record or stop a macro.

▤ Double-click the header/footer in Page Layout view to activate it. To exit, double-click outside of it.

▤ Double-click the left side of the Status Bar to open the Go To dialog box.

Trademark / Copyright

Type (tm) for the trademark symbol.
Type (c) for the copyright symbol.

Drawing Tools

1. Display the Drawing toolbar if necessary (refer to page 22 for help on displaying toolbars).

2. Click on the desired drawing tool.

3. Hold it over your document, and click and drag to draw.

▤ To draw straight lines, hold down the Shift key as you drag.

▤ To draw several objects, double-click the drawing tool, and draw one after the other, as many as you need. To cancel the drawing tool, press Esc.

AutoShapes Several shapes are available on the Drawing toolbar as shown here. The callouts throughout this document were created this way.

1. Click AutoShapes on the Drawing toolbar.
2. Point to Callouts, and click your choice.
3. Hold the mouse pointer (now a crosshair) over your document page, and click and drag out your shape.

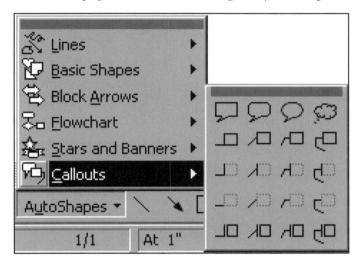

Make sure you review the other AutoShapes options.

Nudge Objects Closer When you're trying to put objects together, you might need one to inch its way closer to the other in very tiny increments. The Nudge feature helps you do this.

1. Select the object you want to nudge.
2. Click Draw on the Drawing toolbar/point to Nudge/choose appropriate direction.

Grouping Objects

This feature lets you group separate objects as one. Examples of this are throughout this book (screen captures and callouts were created as separate pieces, then grouped as one).

1. Click the Selection tool (the solid, white arrow) on the Drawing toolbar (display toolbar if needed).

2. Click and drag a selection box around all the objects you want to group together. You must include all of an object in order for it to become selected.

> The selection box is almost imaginary. It disappears once it's done its job.

3. Release the mouse, and you'll see all objects have been selected. Make sure you selected all of them.

4. Click Draw/Group (or right-click the object for the shortcut menu).

Later, if you need to make changes to any one piece of the grouped object, you'll have to Ungroup it.

1. Click the object until you see the white selection boxes around it.

2. Click Draw/Ungroup/click off the object to deselect everything/make your changes.

3. Repeat Grouping steps to Regroup when finished.

Note: *In the PowerPoint chapter, you'll learn how you can take clipart, convert it to a Microsoft Object, ungroup it, recolor it, steal pieces from it, duplicate it, and more.*

Placement Order

When drawing objects, you will sometimes end up with one piece hiding the other.

1. Display the Drawing toolbar/select the object you want to change the order of.
2. Click Draw, point to Order, and choose.

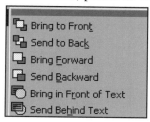

Shadow Settings

Word comes with several tools to help you take a simple object and make it appear to pop off the page. One tool is the Shadow Settings.

1. Click on the Rectangle object on the Drawing toolbar/draw the object, and select it.
2. Click the Shadow Settings toolbar button/click the look you want.

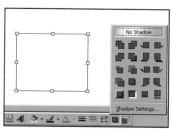

3-D Settings

You can repeat the steps above to give your object a 3-D effect by clicking the 3-D toolbar button once the object is selected.

Typing International Characters

If you type international names often, you can have AutoCorrect replace the English version of what you type with its international version. Use the chart below to type the international characters.

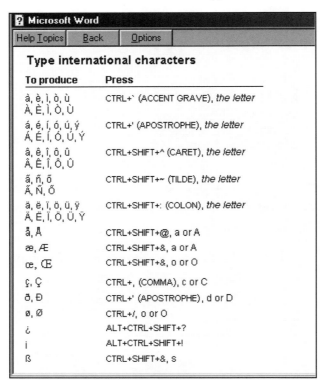

1. Type the international version of the name using the symbols above, and select it.

2. Click Tools/AutoCorrect/AutoCorrect tab/check the Replace text as you type box if not already done so.

3. In the Replace box, type the English version of the name.

4. The international version of the name is in the With box (if you selected the name before you clicked Tools)/click OK.

Graphical Typefaces

If you type the character "a" and change the font to Transport MT, you get a

🚐. Any formatting you apply to regular text can be applied to these. They are not graphics. Your software has more (computer system fonts may vary).

Character	Wingdings 2	Holidays	Transport MT	Vacation	Bon Appetit
a					
b					
c					
d					
e					
f					
g					
h					
i					
j					
k					
l					
m					
n					
o					
p					
q					
r					
s					
t					
u					
v					
w					
x					
y					
z					

Graphical Typefaces, cont'd

Character	Monotype Sorts	Wingdings	Wingdings 2	Wingdings 3	Zapf Dingbats
1	☞	📁	📄	↔	☞
2	●	📄	📋	↕	●
3	✓	📄	🗑	←	✓
4	✓	📄	▭	→	✔
5	✗	📄	▭	↑	✗
6	✖	⌛	🖨	↓	✖
7	✗	⌨	🖨	↯	✗
8	✗	🖱	⊙	↵	✗
9	✚	🖲	📼	↳	✚
0	✎	💼	▢	↨	✎
-	✍	📫	▤	↖	✍
=	†	💾	◌	↱	†
[	✳	☯	&	⇨	✳
]	✾	❀	?	⇨	✾
;	✜	⌨	✎	↪	✜
'	▢	❻	🕐	←	
,	✙	📬	📄	↓	✌
.	✏	📫	📄	↘	✏
/	●	📪	▯	↕	●
<	✜	💾	👆	⌐	✜
>	✝	⊛	✌	⌐	✝
?	†	✍	☞	⌐	†
:	✚	💻	✎	↩	✚
"	✂	✂	✒	→	
{	❜	❀	❼	◣	❜
}	❞	❞	❾	▶	❞

Just Show Me
Which Button
to Click!

EXCEL 97

WORK BOOK

A workbook is similar to a 3-ring binder with tabs. It contains multiple sheets (Sheet1, Sheet2, Sheet3, etc.) that can be renamed, copied, removed, or rearranged. Each workbook contains 255 sheets.

Worksheet

The worksheet is the main Excel document for entering and calculating data. The worksheet contains 256 columns and 65,536 rows. Worksheets can contain more than one page.

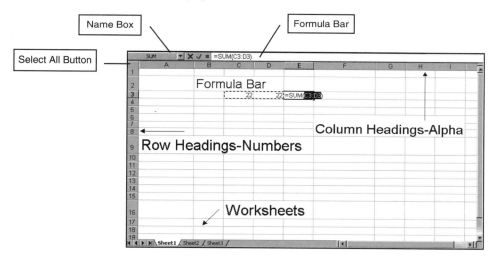

Moving Worksheets

You can reorder worksheets within the workbook:

1. Click the sheet tab you want to move.
2. Drag it over or back to its new location.

Renaming Worksheets

You can rename the Sheet tabs:

1. Point the mouse at the sheet tab to be renamed, and right-click/click Rename/rename the sheet/press Enter.

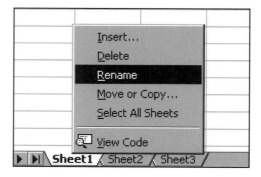

Selecting Cells

Select cells, ranges, rows, and columns:

A single cell: Click the cell, or press the arrow keys, or tab.

A range of cells: Click the first cell in the range and drag to the last cell of the range.

All cells in a worksheet: Click the Select All button (see page 103 diagram of worksheet), or press Ctrl+A.

Nonadjacent cells or cell ranges: Select the first cell in the range, then hold down Ctrl, and select the others.

A large range of cells: Click the first cell, then hold down the Shift key, and click the last cell in the range.

An entire row: Click the row heading (the number label).

An entire column: Click the column heading (the letter label).

Mouse Pointers

The mouse pointer takes on several shapes depending upon its function. The mouse pointer **must** take on these shapes first before the function can be performed.

Select Cells — Large plus sign

Move Cells — Arrow

Copy Cells — Arrow with tiny plus sign

Change Column Width — Vertical bar with horizontal arrows

Once the pointer is in the position as shown, double-clicking the border will automatically adjust the column to fit the longest line of text you have entered. The same applies below for the row.

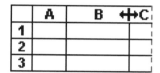

Changing Row Height — Horizontal bar with vertical arrows

AutoFill — Medium plus sign +

Editing Text — I-Beam

EXCEL

Cell Reference

Excel labels columns with letters (A through IV for a total of 256 columns), and labels rows with numbers (1 through 65,536). The location of a cell is called its cell reference.

To refer to a cell, enter the column letter followed by the row number (B1). Below, the cell reference for the active cell is B1. Column "B" intersects with row "1."

To refer to a range of cells, enter the reference for the cell in the upper-left corner of the range, a colon (:), and then put the reference for the cell in the lower-right corner of the range.

Example of Cell Reference: A1:C3, cells A1 through C3.

If the cell reference is on a different worksheet within the workbook, designate the cell as Sheetname!A1, where Sheetname is whatever you named the worksheet you're referring to.

Relative / Absolute Cell Reference

Reference to a cell's location is either a relative reference or absolute. Knowing the difference is important when you're copying formulas to other locations.

More information on relative and absolute references begins on page 127.

FILE

Toolbar buttons

Hold mouse pointer under each toolbar button to see what it does. To display additional toolbars, point the mouse anywhere on a toolbar, right-click, and click your choice.

Page Setup

1. Click File/Page Setup. From here, you can change the margins, header/footer, sheet size, and layout.

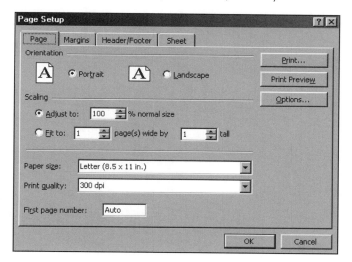

Aligning Page

To align the worksheet on the printed page horizontally or vertically:

1. Click File/Page Setup/Margins tab.
2. Check Horizontally or Vertically.

Repeating Row Labels on Pages

Instead of typing column titles on every page within your worksheet, designate the row you want repeated after each page break.

1. Click File/Page Setup/Sheet tab.

2. Click inside the "Rows to repeat at top" text box/click the Collapse Dialog Box button on the right of the text box so the dialog box will be out of your way.

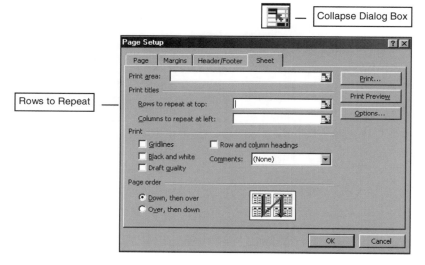

3. Select the row in your worksheet that you want repeated on every page after each page break.

4. Click the Collapse Dialog Box again to restore it to its original size/OK.

Printing Gridlines

If you want the gridlines on your spreadsheet to print:

1. Click File/Page Setup/Sheet tab/check the Gridlines check box/click OK.

EDIT

Paste Special

Paste Special is used when you want to paste only part of a cell's attributes or to paste links.

1. Copy the cell or range that has data you want to paste elsewhere/right-click the cell in which you will paste the data/click Paste Special/make choices/OK.

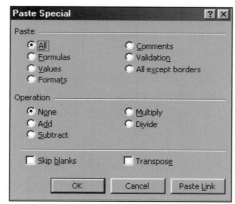

Select the characteristics you want transferred:

- **All**. Transfers everything.
- **Formulas**. Transfers only the formulas.
- **Values**. Transfers only the values and formula results.
- **Formats**. Transfers only cell formats.
- **Comments**. Transfers only comments.

The **Operation** options allow you to determine how you want the transferred information combined with the cells being pasted into (i.e., Add to, Subtract from).

Check the **Skip Blanks** check box if you do not want to paste blank cells on top of existing cell contents. Check **Transpose** to change rows to columns or vice versa.

Paste Link   Once you create text or a formula that you want to use in other cells, pasting them as links keeps them tied together. When the original cell changes, so does the linked cell.

To paste a link, follow the steps for Paste Special on page 109, and click the Paste Link button as shown on the diagram.

Note: *You'll learn more about formulas beginning on page 125.*

Delete Command   The Delete command under the Edit menu deletes the entire cell from the worksheet. To delete contents of a cell, use the Clear command.

Center Text over Cells   To type a title or other data above several cells, you can quickly merge the cells and automatically center the title over the text.

1. Select the cells where you want the title to appear.
2. Click the Merge and Center toolbar button, and type your text (you can realign text if desired).

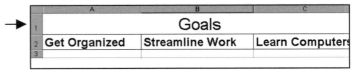

	A	B	C
1		Goals	
2	Get Organized	Streamline Work	Learn Computer
3			

Entering Data   1. Click the cell to select it (or tab to it)/type the data.
2. Press Enter or Tab or click off the cell so data is entered.

Note: *If data is already in the cell, double-click inside the cell to edit data, or select the cell and press F2.*

Shortcuts for Entering Data

▤ To quickly fill in the active cell with the contents of the cell above it, press Ctrl+D.

▤ To fill in the active cell with the contents of the cell to the left of it, press CTRL+R.

Cut-Copy-Paste

This feature works the same as explained in the Word chapter. But in Excel, when a cell or range has been cut or copied, the action is indicated by a moving border.

1. Select the cell with the data you want to cut or copy.

2. Click the Cut or Copy toolbar button. A moving border will appear around the cell.

3. Select the target cell, and Paste or Paste Special the cell contents into the target cell.

4. Press Esc to remove the moving border.

Go To a Cell

To go to a particular cell quickly:

1. Press Ctrl+G (or press F5), and type the cell number in the Reference box.

Repeat a Command

1. Press Ctrl+Y to repeat a command (does not repeat typing).

EXCEL

Clear Command

To clear everything in a cell, select the cell or range of cells, and press the Delete key. To choose what you want to delete from a cell, use the Clear command.

1. Select the cell or range of cells in which you want to clear contents/click Edit/Clear/make your choice.

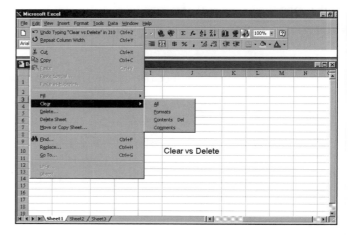

▤ **All**. Clears everything.

▤ **Formats**. Clears only the formatting.

▤ **Contents**. Clears the contents, but leaves formatting.

▤ **Comments**. Clears comments you've added.

Note: *Do not select a cell and then use the space bar to clear its contents. A space will be left in the cell and can cause calculation problems.*

AutoFill

With AutoFill, you can copy the value of a cell to other cells in the same row or column in increments. For example, if a cell contains "January," you can quickly fill in the other cells in a row or column with the series, "February, March, April" and so on.

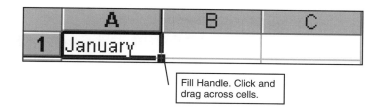

Fill Handle. Click and drag across cells.

EXCEL

Built-In Series

Excel has several built-in AutoFill series.

1. Type January in the first cell/point to the fill handle (the black square) until the pointer turns into a medium plus sign.

2. Click and drag the fill handle across the other cells in the same row. The other months of the year will automatically appear.

Note: *To see other built-in series, click Tools/Options/click the Custom Lists tab.*

Prevent Series Increments

To have Excel repeat the information you've typed into a cell(s) without incrementing:

1. Select the cell or range of cells that have the data you want to repeat.

2. Hold down the Ctrl key, and drag the fill handle across the other cells in the same row(s) or down the same column(s).

Example: You want January, February, March repeated across all cells instead of all months of the year.

Creating Your Own AutoFill Series

If you have a series of information you use often, like a list of cities in your area, you can create your own AutoFill series.

1. Type the data for the series into the cells.
2. Select the data/click Tools/Options/click the Custom Lists tab.

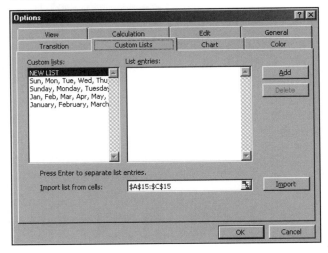

3. Click Import/OK.

Note: *Remember that when you want to call up the series later, just type the first word in the series (or any word if you don't want the entire series) into a cell, grab the fill handle, and drag.*

Creating AutoFill Series from Scratch

If you don't already have data in cells to copy as part of a series, you can create one easily from scratch.

1. Click Tools/Options.
2. Click the Custom Lists tab.
3. Type your entries into the List entries text box, pressing Enter to separate each one.
4. Click Add when finished/OK.

Creating a Series of Numbers

You can fill a range of cells with a series of numbers.

1. Enter the starting number in the first cell.
2. Enter the next value into the next cell in whatever increment you want (i.e., put 10 in the first cell and 15 in the second).
3. Select the two cells/drag the fill handle over the adjacent cells to fill them/release the mouse.

Using AutoFill with Formulas

AutoFill can be used to quickly copy formulas to other cells.

See more information on formulas beginning on page 125.

EXCEL

VIEW

Header and Footer

1. Click View/Header and Footer.

2. Click the Custom Header button (or Footer).

3. Click in a section, and type desired information.

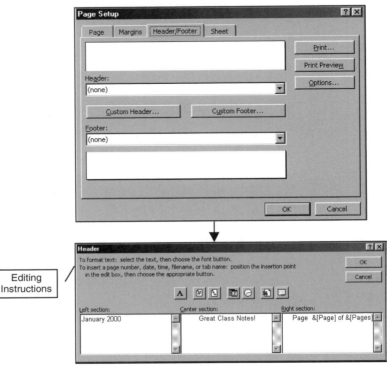

Editing Instructions

Font Command and Special Inserts

To insert a page number, date, time, filename, or sheet tab name:

1. Click inside either section (Left, Center, or Right)/click the appropriate button.

To format text in the header/footer:

2. Select the text/click font button (A) /make changes/click OK until you're back in your document/click Print Preview to see layout.

INSERT

Page Break

Inserting a page break keeps you in the same worksheet, just on a different page in the worksheet. Excel inserts page breaks automatically. You can also insert them manually.

1. Select the row immediately after the row where you want the break (Row 4 in this case) /click Insert/Page Break (page breaks indicated by dotted lines).

	A	B	C
1			
2	John	Roberts	Atlanta
3	Mary	Johnson	CPark
4	Steven	Darnell	Stn Mtn
5	Mae	Keith	Roswell
6	Brad	Neal	
7			

Remove a Page Break

To remove a Page Break:

1. Select the row after the Page Break line/click Insert/Remove Page Break.

Insert Cells/Rows/Columns

1. Right-click a cell, row heading, or column heading/click Insert.

If you select a row heading, another row will be added. If you select a column heading, another column will be added. Select two, and Excel will add two, and so on.

Insert Worksheet

1. Right-click a sheet tab/click Insert/Worksheet.

Comments

You can add comments to cells in your worksheet for others to review:

1. Select the cell/click Insert/Comments/type your comments.

    Note: *Cells with comments inserted have a red arrow in the upper-right corner. To view comments, hold the mouse pointer over the arrow.*

Charts

You can take the data in your spreadsheet and create all sorts of picture representations of it by creating charts.

Note: *Only the basics of creating a chart are discussed in this book. Refer to the Suggested Reading list in the back of this book for a reference with more details on advanced charting.*

The Data

To understand how charting works, you have to first understand the layout of the data in the table, and how it translates to the chart. Selecting the right data in the table is crucial to creating a chart that will make sense.

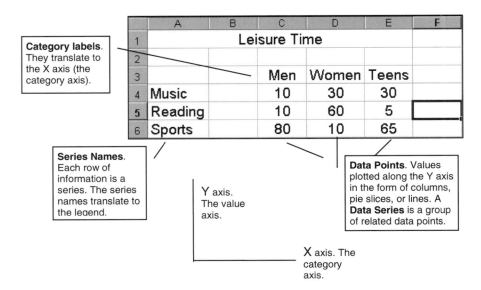

Category labels. They translate to the X axis (the category axis).

	A	B	C	D	E	F
1	Leisure Time					
2						
3			Men	Women	Teens	
4	Music		10	30	30	
5	Reading		10	60	5	
6	Sports		80	10	65	

Series Names. Each row of information is a series. The series names translate to the legend.

Y axis. The value axis.

Data Points. Values plotted along the Y axis in the form of columns, pie slices, or lines. A **Data Series** is a group of related data points.

X axis. The category axis.

Parts of a Chart

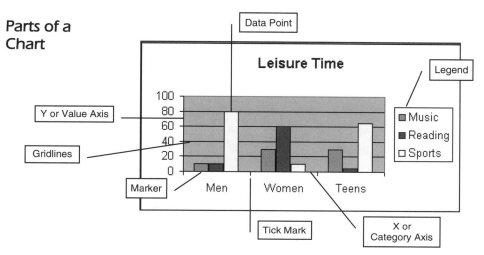

Data Point

Legend

Leisure Time

Y or Value Axis

Gridlines

■ Music
■ Reading
□ Sports

Marker

Men   Women   Teens

Tick Mark

X or Category Axis

Chart Terms

▣ **Axis**. Forms the boundaries of the chart and contains the scale for plotting data.

– The **Y axis** (or the value axis) is the vertical axis.

– The **X axis** (or the category axis) is the horizontal axis.

▣ **Data Point**. A single piece of data, such as the number of men who listened to music for leisure.

▣ **Data Series**. A collection of data points, such as all the people who enjoyed reading as a leisure activity. Each data series has a unique color or pattern (pie charts have only one data series).

▣ **Gridlines**. Lines you add to make it easier to view data.

▣ **Legend**. A guide outside the chart that explains the symbols, patterns, or colors used to distinguish the different data series.

▣ **Marker**. An object that represents a data point, such as bars, pies, etc.

▣ **Plot Area**. Rectangular area bounded by the two axes.

▣ **Tick Mark**. A division mark along the x and y axes.

**Chart
Wizard**

The Chart Wizard is a series of dialog boxes that guide you through the steps involved in creating an embedded chart. (Details follow on next page.)

1. Select the data you want to chart/click the Chart Wizard toolbar button.

2. Click the Chart type and Chart sub-type.

3. Click *and hold down* the Press and Hold to View Sample button to see if you've selected the right data/release the button after viewing/click Next if satisfied.

4. Decide if you want the data charted by Row or by Column/click Next. (See page 121.)

5. Change Chart Options, including chart title, titles for X and Y axis, etc./click Next. (See page 122.)

6. Decide if you want the chart to be placed in a separate document or in the worksheet with the selected data (called an embedded chart) /click Finish.

7. Drag the chart to its new location. Hold down Alt as you drag the chart to align it with a cell edge.

Note: *Once you create the chart, every time the data changes, the chart is updated automatically. If it doesn't, click Tools/Options/Calculation/choose Automatic/OK.*

Also, if you add another data series to your worksheet later, select it, grab the border of the selected cells, and drag it over to your chart and drop it. The chart will automatically update to include the new data.

Charting Data

The data series, a collection of associated data, can be plotted by row or by column. Let's look at the Leisure Time worksheet again.

	A	B	C	D	E
1	Leisure Time				
2					
3			Men	Women	Teens
4	Music		10	30	30
5	Reading		10	60	5
6	Sports		80	10	65

Charting Data by Row

Charting by row plots data based on row titles. The row titles in the table above are Music, Reading, and Sports. The row titles translated to the legend as shown below.

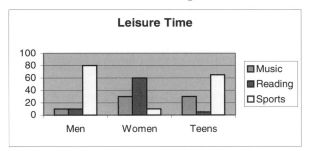

Charting Data by Column

Charting by column plots data based on column titles.

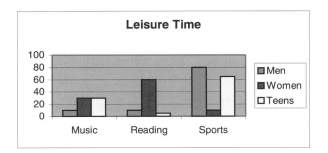

Chart Options

During the Chart Wizard process, you have the opportunity to modify Chart Options and add titles, data labels, and more.

Note: If you've finished the chart and you want to get to this dialog box, right-click outside the plot area, and click Chart Options.

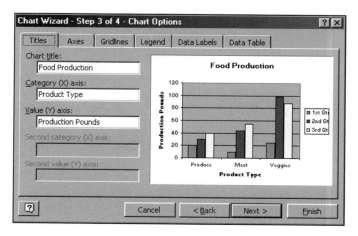

1. **Titles**. Add titles to the chart and the axes.

2. **Axes**. Set your primary axis for x and y.

3. **Gridlines**. Decide which gridlines you want to print in your chart. (To turn these off later, right-click on one/click Clear.)

4. **Legend**. Determine placement of your legend.

5. **Data Labels**. Have label names listed.

6. **Data Table**. Place data table at the bottom of your chart.

Chart Styles   If you're always creating the same style of chart and tweaking it to your style (i.e., font, colors, and so on), you could instead create a chart style and store it as Excel's default chart style.

1. Create a chart as you normally would, tweaking it as described above.

2. Once the chart is created, select it/click Chart/Chart Type/click Custom Types tab. Your chart will display in the preview window.

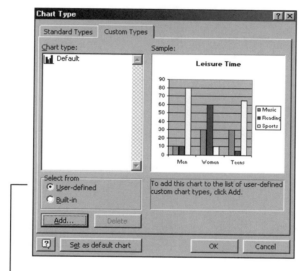

3. In the Select from box, click User-defined/Add.

4. Type in a name and description/click OK/Set as Default Chart/Yes.

Creating the Default Chart

If you create the same types of chart often, you can let Excel create a chart quickly based on the default chart. Once the chart is created, you can use the chart commands to change it if needed.

If you want to create a default chart in a different worksheet:

1. Select the data you want charted/press F11.

   A new tab is added to your workbook for the chart. You can copy the chart and paste it to another location and resize it. Right-click on the chart to modify it.

If you want to create a chart based on the default and keep the chart with the worksheet.

1. Select the data you want charted/click the Chart Wizard toolbar button/click Finish/right-click on the chart to modify it if needed.

Pictures as Data Markers

You can use pictures as data markers in your column and bar charts. **Example:** You could have data charted with pictures of vegetables.

1. Click the data marker on the chart that you want to replace/click the Fill Color drop-down arrow on the Drawing toolbar/Fill Effects/Picture tab.

2. Select Picture/browse for picture you want, and double-click it/change desired options/click OK.

Note: See Help for more details on this feature (under pictures).

Formulas

A formula is a sequence of values, cell references, functions, or operators that can produce a new value from existing values. Formulas are the basis for Excel's power.

Creating Formulas

A formula always begins with an = sign, and is either entered in the cell or in the formula bar. A colon (:) acts as a range operator and is used as you would the word "through." Cell A8:D8 is like saying cells A8 through D8.

The operators Excel uses are as follows:

+ Add
- Subtraction
* Multiplication
/ Division
% Percentage
^ Exponentiation (to the power of)

The example below is a formula that adds values in Column D, Row 8 through Column G, Row 8.

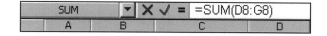

To enter a formula in a worksheet:

1. Click the cell in which you want to enter a formula.

2. Type an = sign and the formula/press Enter or click the green check. (**Example**: =A1*G2 will multiply Column A, Row 1 by Column G, Row 2.)

Note: *Refer to Help or the Suggested Reading list in the back of this book for a reference with more details on formulas.*

**Errors in
Formulas**

When a formula can't evaluate the result, Excel will
display the following error values.

######. Calculated data was too large for the cell.

#VALUE. The wrong type of argument or operand is
used in the formula. Arguments are the values a function
uses to perform calculations or operations (numeric
values, cell references, ranges of cells, etc.).

#REF!. Cell reference is not valid.

#NUM!. There is a problem with a number in a formula
or function.

#NULL!. When you create a formula that includes cell
ranges that don't intersect. If the cells don't intersect, you
have to use a comma to separate the ranges. For example,
SUM(A1:A5,B2:B8).

#NAME?. Excel doesn't recognize text in the formula.

#N/A. Value is not available to a function or formula. If
you have a cell that will hold data that is not yet available,
type #N/A in the cell so Excel won't try to calculate it.

#DIV/0!. A formula is dividing by zero.

***Note**: To view all formulas in your spreadsheet, press Ctrl+~ (cells
will expand to show longer formulas). Repeat the steps to change
spreadsheet back.*

Copying Formulas

When copying formulas or using AutoFill to copy a formula to other locations, you'll need to understand the difference in absolute reference and relative reference when referring to a cell's location.

Relative Reference

The default in Excel is to write all formulas with relative reference. This means that cell references change when you copy the formula to a new location or when you fill a range with a formula.

In the following example, Mary, John, and Joe received a bonus amount and a cost of living increase amount that will be added to their monthly salary. The regular salary and the bonus amount were added to form a new salary. Then, the cost of living increase was applied.

The formula that would multiply their new salary (D6) by the cost of living increase (C3) was entered as D6*C3 in cell E6. When the formula was copied down to the other cells in Column E, the formula for each cell changed to D7**C4** and D8**C5**. These formulas obviously produced incorrect results. Why? Because the cost of living increase was **only** in cell C3, and not cell C4 or C5.

E6		=D6*C3			
A	B	C	D	E	F
1		Employee Salary Increases			
2					
3 Cost of Living Increase		4%			
4					
5	$ Salary	Bonus	$ Total	$ Cost of Living	Total
6 Mary	30,000	6.00%	1,800.00	72.00	1,872.00
7 John	50,000	5.00%	2,500.00	-	2,500.00
8 Joe	80,000	3.00%	2,400.00	#VALUE!	#VALUE!

To make sure you understand this concept, duplicate this spreadsheet in Excel and walk through the steps.

Absolute Reference

When you need the address of the cell to stay the same as you copy a formula to another location, you'll need to designate the cell reference as absolute. You do this by placing dollar signs in front of both the column letter and the row number (i.e., C3).

Continuing with the same example, see what happens when an absolute cell reference for cell C3 is used in the formula in Column E instead of a relative reference.

The cell address, C3 (the 4% cost of living increase), was entered into the formula as an absolute reference because as the formula in cell E6 is copied down to other cells in Column E, the cell address, C3, needed to absolutely stay the same.

The absolute cell reference C3 says each amount in column D will **always** be multiplied by the cell address of C3.

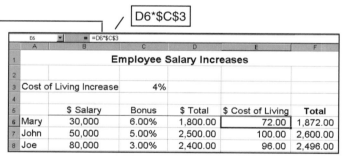

D6*C3

	A	B	C	D	E	F
1			Employee Salary Increases			
2						
3	Cost of Living Increase		4%			
4						
5		$ Salary	Bonus	$ Total	$ Cost of Living	Total
6	Mary	30,000	6.00%	1,800.00	72.00	1,872.00
7	John	50,000	5.00%	2,500.00	100.00	2,600.00
8	Joe	80,000	3.00%	2,400.00	96.00	2,496.00

Note: When a formula has already been created and you want to change its reference type, click inside the formula on the formula bar, and press F4 until it becomes the format you want.

Reference Cells in a Different Worksheet

You can reference cells in different worksheets within the same workbook by adding the sheetname to the formula.

=A3*Expenses!D4.

Note: Don't overlook the exclamation point following the sheetname.

Insert Function

To perform math functions such as an average:

1. Click in the cell directly next to or under the column or row you want an average for.

2. Click Insert/Function (or click the Function toolbar button).

3. Choose the AVERAGE function to produce an average of the numbers in the selected cells/click OK/OK.

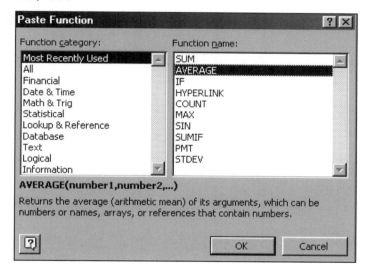

AutoSum

You can quickly add a column or row by clicking the AutoSum button. Use only when values are directly above or to the left of the cell where you want the total.

1. Click in the cell directly next to or under the column or row to total.

2. Click the AutoSum toolbar button/press Enter.

FORMAT

Styles

You learned the concept of styles in the Word chapter. Excel has a version of styles that you can apply to cells. If there is a particular number format, alignment, font, etc., you use often, you can create a style and apply it to the cells in your document.

1. Click Format/Style/type a new file name for your style/click Modify and format/click Add/OK.

Fills and Colors

To change a cell's fill pattern, or recolor text and lines:

1. Select the cell, row, column, text, or line you want to recolor.

2. Click the appropriate toolbar button on the Drawing toolbar (display if needed).

Format Cells

To change the format of data in a cell:

1. Right-click the cell/click Format Cells.

2. Select the desired tab.

Format Cells for Currency

You can quickly format cells for currency and decrease or increase decimal places.

1. Right-click the cell to format/click Format Cells/Number tab/Currency category/choose settings.

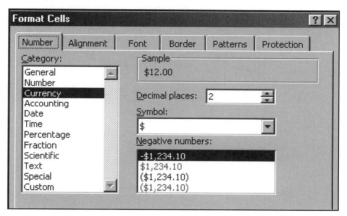

You can quickly format cells for currency and percentage, and also change decimal places by using the corresponding toolbar buttons.

1. Select the cell to format/click the appropriate toolbar button.

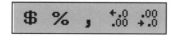

Special Formatting

You can format a cell (and column or row) for zip codes (and zip code+4), phone numbers, Social Security numbers.

1. Right-click the cell, column, or row/click Format Cells/click the Special category/choose type/OK.

Note: *Once the cell is formatted, type the number without any spaces or dashes. Excel will format it automatically.*

Cell Borders To format the cell's borders:

1. Right-click the cell to be formatted/click Format
    Cells/the Border tab/make the appropriate choices.

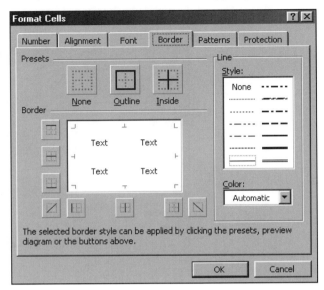

The selected border style can be applied by clicking:

   ▤ Presets

   ▤ Preview Diagram

   ▤ Border buttons

Example: You want a border to print on the bottom of a
selected cell. You would:

1. Click inside the Preview Diagram, and click the
    bottom of the diagram's box.

You can also click to change the style and color of a line.
To erase the border, click on it again.

Text Alignment in Cells

You can change the direction of the text in a cell and choose where the information will set (at top of cell, bottom, center, etc.).

Sometimes you'll also need to have text wrap inside a cell.

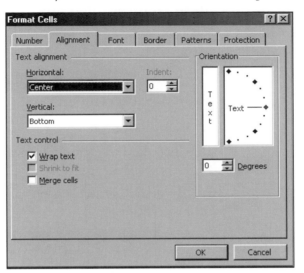

1. Right-click the cell with data to be formatted/click Format Cells/Alignment tab.

Note: If you only see the Font tab, it means you have typed data in the cell, but you didn't press Enter or click off the cell so data would be entered. Close the dialog box/click off the cell/repeat Step 1.

2. Click drop-down arrows for Horizontal or Vertical, and choose how text will set inside the cell.

3. Check the Wrap text in the Text control box if desired.

To change the direction of the data in the cell:

4. Click inside the degree diagram to depict how you want the text to flow, or change in the Degrees box.

TOOLS

Protection

By default, the cells in an Excel worksheet are locked. The locked cell status has no effect unless the sheet is protected. If you unlock certain cells, and then protect the sheet, you will only be able to tab to the unlocked cells. This feature is great if you're creating a form and only want users to tab to the cells that require data.

Create your worksheet so you'll know which cells to unlock. Then:

1. Right-click on the cell to unlock/click Format Cells.

2. Click the Protection tab/clear the Locked check box. Repeat for all appropriate cells.

3. Then, protect the sheet: click Tools/Protection/ Protect Sheet.

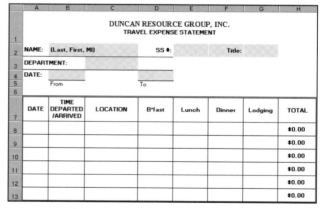

This is a sample of part of a travel expense statement. Once the sheet is protected, you can only tab to and enter data into the cells that require information. **Example:** When tabbing, you'll bypass the Name cell. But when you tab to the (Last, First, MI) cell, you'll be able to type in it because it was unlocked before the sheet was protected.

Sharing a Workbook

If you're on a network, you can share your workbook with others, have them make suggested changes, track changes each reviewer makes, and decide whether to keep the changes or not.

To select the users who will review the workbook:

1. Open the workbook/click Tools/Share Workbook/click the Editing tab and click the check box to have more than one user make changes/click the Advanced tab to set more options/OK.

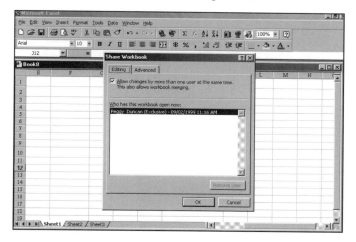

Note: *To unshare a workbook, repeat the steps above but stop after you click the Editing tab. In the "Who has this workbook open now" box, click the name of the user you want to disconnect, and then click Remove User.*

Some of the features in Excel will not be available when a workbook is shared. It's best to complete the workbook as much as possible before you share it. To see a list of limitations:

1. Click Help/Contents and Index/Index tab/type "shared workbooks" in the text box/double-click Limitations.

Track Changes

You'll want to know who made which suggestions for changes, and you'll want the option of not accepting the changes. When you use the Highlight Changes command, Excel highlights the following changes:

- Changes to cell contents, including moved and pasted contents.

- Inserted and deleted rows and columns.

1. Open the workbook/click Tools/point to Track Changes/click Highlight Changes/make choices/OK.

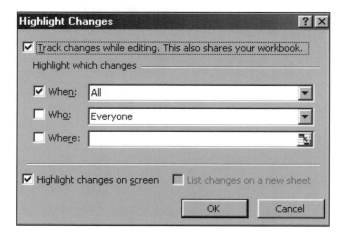

For additional help on tracking changes:

1. Click Help/Contents and Index/Index tab/type "shared workbooks" in the text box/double-click Editing.

DATA

Sort

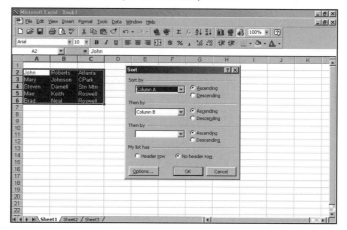

It's easy to sort or rearrange data.

1. Select data to sort/click Data /Sort.

If you select only one column of data before sorting, you'll get a dialog box asking if you want to expand the selection.

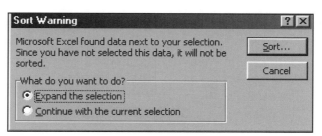

2. Click OK to expand the selection (this means that all data associated with the entry you have selected will stay together).

For simple sorts, select the data to be sorted, and click the Sort Ascending or Descending toolbar button.

Filter Data

If you use Excel to manage a database list, you can filter the list so it shows a particular group of records. **Example:** You might have 200 names and addresses in your database, and you want to filter out all the people living in the city of Durham.

1. With your database document open, click inside a cell/click Data/point to Filter/click AutoFilter.

2. Click the down-pointing arrow next to the City column/click Durham.

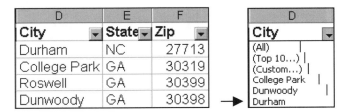

3. All residents of Durham who are in your database will appear in a filtered list (click All to unfilter later.)

Form Command

Another feature that will help you manage a database in Excel is the Form command. The Form command lets you view records in your database as one column of data.

1. Click inside a cell of your database/click Data/Form.

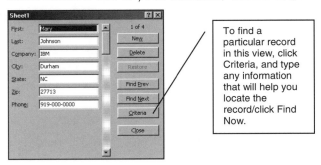

To find a particular record in this view, click Criteria, and type any information that will help you locate the record/click Find Now.

WINDOW

Freeze Panes

When you're scrolling through your spreadsheet, you'll often want to know what the column and row titles are so you can determine which record you're viewing.

You can freeze the windowpane so that no matter how far down or across on the page you scroll, this information will always be in view.

To freeze panes:

1. Click next to the row and under the column you want to freeze.
2. Click Window/Freeze Panes.

In this case, once the pane is frozen, Row 1 and Columns A and B will always be in view, regardless of how you scroll.

Unfreeze Panes

To unfreeze panes, repeat the steps, but click Unfreeze Panes.

Just Show Me
Which Button
to Click!

POWERPOINT® 97

GETTING STARTED

With PowerPoint, you can create a winning presentation consisting of eye-popping transparencies, or a multimedia event complete with movies and sound. You can get started several ways.

- **AutoContent Wizard.** Define what you want to say and how you will say it with the built-in content.
- **Template.** Base the presentation on a built-in template.
- **Blank presentation.** Start out with a blank presentation and build it from scratch.

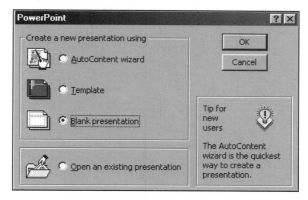

AutoLayout

Above, the "Blank presentation" option was selected.

1. Double-click one of the AutoLayouts.

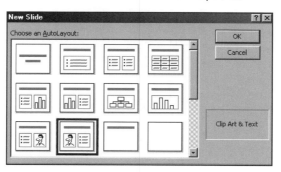

FILE

New Presentation

If you're already in PowerPoint and you want to create a new presentation:

1. Click File/New/choose one of the built-in templates/click OK.

You can change the look of your presentation in various ways. You'll learn how easy it is later in this chapter.

Page Setup

1. Click File/Page Setup. From here, you can change the margins, page size, and layout.

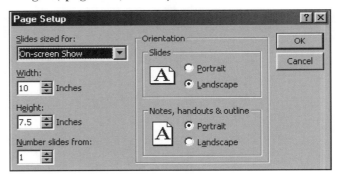

Print Options

You can vary what you want to print and how you want PowerPoint to print your slides.

1. Click File/Print/click the Print What box drop-down arrow/choose desired options.

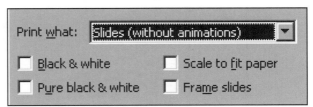

EDIT

Most of the Edit features in PowerPoint work the same as in Word, and are not repeated in this chapter.

VIEW

Slide Views

1. Click View/make your selection.

Slide View takes you to the actual slide so you can edit.

Outline View shows an outline of your presentation. You can edit and change the slide order around easily in this view. To change the order, just click the slide indicator and drag.

Slide Sorter View shows you all the slides at a glance. This is where you will change how your slide and bullets appear during the slide show. Move the slide order around by clicking the slide and dragging to new location.

Notes Pages View displays a box to use for special notations.

Slide Show View shows you how your presentation will look and behave during a slide show.

Master View is the master slide that determines how the entire presentation will look.

Black and White View shows how your color presentation will look in black and white.

Slide Miniatures. In slide view, displays a miniature version of your slide. Click the miniature slide to change views or to see transitions and other effects.

Speaker's Notes. This view takes you to a notes page to add notes you can view during the slide show.

POWERPOINT

Slide Changer

The Slide Changer allows you to change views with a mouse click. The Slide Changer is located just above the Status Bar in the bottom left corner of your screen.

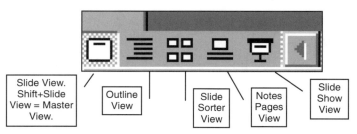

Header and Footer

To have information appear on every slide, put it in the header or footer. In this example, items that will appear on every slide include a fixed date as indicated, the slide number, and the footer text, "Great Class."

1. Click View/Header and Footer/make selections/Apply to current slide or Apply to All.

Note: *To move the location where these items will appear on the slide, see Master Slides on page 148.*

INSERT

New Slide

To insert a new slide into your presentation:

1. Click Insert/New Slide/choose format.

Or

1. Click the New Slide toolbar button.

Note: *To bypass the New Slide selection dialog box, hold down the Shift key before you click the button or the menu item.*

Movies and Sound

1. Click Insert/point to Movies and Sounds/click Movie from Gallery or Movie from File.

Once the .avi (movie) or .midi (music), etc., files are embedded, you'll have to adjust settings that determine when and how they will play in your presentation. (See Multimedia section for these instructions beginning on page 157.)

Clip Art

1. Click Insert/point to Picture/click Clip Art.

Or

1. Click the Insert Clip Art toolbar button.
   Find out how to edit Clip Art on page 165.

Comments

You can insert comment boxes right on your slide.

1. Click Insert/Comment/type the comment.

To hide the Comment box:

1. Click View/Comments.

Note: *Display the Reviewing toolbar/format the Comments box as you would any other object, changing AutoShape, fill color, etc.*

POWERPOINT

FORMAT

Line Spacing

1. Click Format/Line Spacing/change space between lines or before and after paragraphs.

Or

1. Select the paragraphs to change/click Increase/Decrease Paragraph Spacing toolbar button.

Master Slides

PowerPoint uses *masters* to help maintain consistency in the design of your presentation. Each view has a master associated with it. With your slide presentation, background color, text color, font, font size, and header and footer location should be controlled on the master slide. If you have to change any of these attributes later, you only have to change the master. (The title slide, or cover page, has its own master.)

1. Click View/point to Master/click Slide Master.

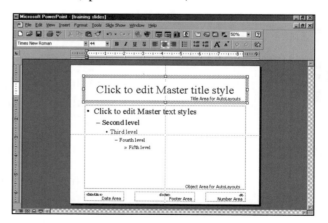

Note: *The text boxes with footer information can be moved around on the slide as you desire. Text that goes into the text boxes is created by going to the Header and Footer command under View (see page 146).*

Apply Design

PowerPoint comes with lots of built-in templates that have been professionally designed.

1. From Master view, click Format/Apply Design (or click the Apply Design toolbar button).

2. Use the keyboard up/down arrow to view each design.

3. Make your selection/click Apply.

Slide Color Scheme

Professionally-designed color schemes also come with PowerPoint.

1. From Master view, click Format/Slide Color Scheme/choose scheme.

2. Click the Custom tab to view what each element will look like.

The Tips for New Users box displays information on how to choose a color scheme.

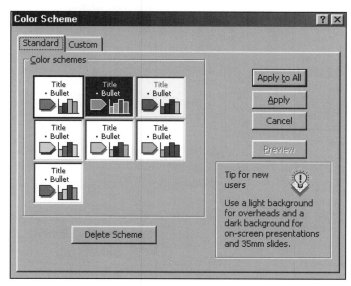

POWERPOINT

Slide Background

It is best to use the professionally-designed color schemes that come with PowerPoint. However, you can change the background color and fill effect of your slide.

1. In Master view, click Format/Background.

2. Click on the color box drop-down arrow/Fill Effects/click the different tabs to see all the possibilities.

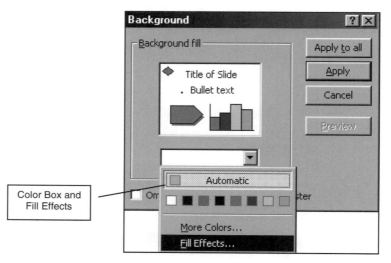

Color Box and Fill Effects

Slide Layout

You can change the AutoLayout option of a slide.

1. In slide view, click the AutoLayout toolbar button.

Change Font Size

You can use the Increase and Decrease Font Size toolbar buttons to change the size of your text.

1. Select the text to be changed/click the Increase or Decrease Font Size button until text is the right size.

TOOLS

AutoClipArt

PowerPoint can automatically locate clip art that fits the content of your presentation. Once you complete the presentation:

1. In slide view, click Tools/AutoClipArt.

PowerPoint will notify you if it finds images that might work for your presentation.

2. View Clip Art/double-click your choices.

Bookshelf

Microsoft Bookshelf is a multimedia reference of online books and materials you can use to look up information. Microsoft Bookshelf Basics comes with the Professional Edition of Microsoft Office and includes a thesaurus, dictionary, and famous quotations. A more complete version that includes a zip code finder, almanac, world atlas, and more can be ordered as a separate product.

To open Bookshelf Basics:

1. Put your CD-ROM containing your Microsoft Office *Professional Edition* software into the appropriate CD-ROM drive:

2. Click Tools/Look Up Reference. Bookshelf Basics will open/browse all the possibilities.

Note: *If you're not inside a program, click the Start button/point to Programs/point to Microsoft Reference/click Bookshelf Basics.*

Define a Word

To look up the definition of a word:

1. With your Office CD still in the drive, right-click the word/click Define.

POWERPOINT

SLIDE SHOW

Slide Transitions

Note: *Throughout all the following steps, select the slide(s) you want to change, then proceed with the steps.*

You can change the way the slide looks when it comes into view during your slide show by changing the transition.

1. From slide sorter view, click the Slide Transition button (or from slide view, click Slide Show/Transitions).

2. Choose the transition, how long slide will stay in view (Advance), and which sound slides will make during transition/click Apply or Apply to All.

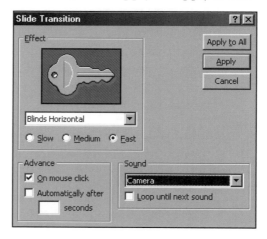

Here, the Blinds Horizontal transition has been chosen, the speed is fast, a camera sound will play during the transition, and clicking the mouse will activate the transition to the next slide.

Note: *To see your results, go to slide show view. Press Esc when finished viewing.*

Text Animation

You can make text or bulleted text appear one paragraph, word, or letter at a time, and dim it after animation. You can also add sounds and transitions.

Animation Effects

Preset animation effects are predefined effects you can quickly apply to your text and title.

1. From slide view, click the Animation Effects toolbar button located on the Formatting toolbar.

2. Click the text in your slide/click one of the Animation Effects buttons. Repeat for slide title.

Custom Animation

You can add additional animation effects to your text or title with the Custom Animation toolbar button.

1. From slide view, click text/click the Custom Animation toolbar button (on the Animation Effects toolbar)/click the Effects tab/make changes.

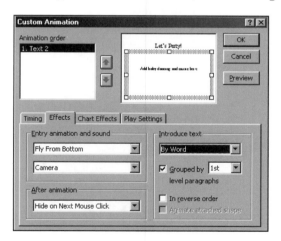

Here, the bulleted text will fly in from the bottom, make a camera sound, disappear after animation (on next mouse click), and will be introduced one word at a time.

Animation
Order

With Custom Animation, you can also change the order
that you want the title and text to appear during the slide
show.

1. From slide view, click the Custom Animation toolbar
   button (as explained previously)/click the Effects tab.

2. In the Animation order box, click the Title or
   Text/click the up or down arrow to rearrange order.

3. Click the Preview button to see the results.

Now, we'll change the timing.

Timing

Timing lets you determine when animation will start for
each embedded object. To change the timing:

1. Continuing from above, click the Timing tab/choose
   whether to start animation on mouse click or so many
   seconds after previous event. You can also choose not
   to animate.

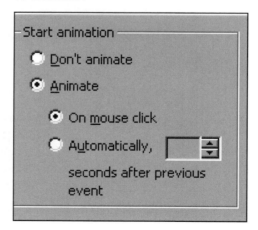

Text Animation Levels

If you have more than one level of indented text, you can determine if you want each level to animate separately or together.

    ▤ This is a 1st level bullet indent.
        ● This is a 2nd level bullet indent.
           - This is a 3rd level bullet indent.

1. From the Animation Effects toolbar, click the Custom Animation toolbar button/Effects tab/choose Effect.

    ▤ If you want the 1st, 2nd, and 3rd level indents to appear on the screen grouped as one paragraph during the slide show, group by 1st level paragraphs.

    ▤ If you want the 1st level indent to appear first. Then, on the next animation, you want all of its sub-bullets to appear, group by 2nd level paragraphs.

    ▤ If you want each of the three level indents to appear independently, group by 3rd level paragraphs.

    ▤ If you don't want animation on any of the levels, choose No Effect. All bullets on that slide will appear at once.

Note: *Both levels have the same animation effect. This step only determines when they will appear on the screen.*

**Animate
Multiple
Slides**

To animate text on multiple slides at once, you'll need to be in slide sorter view. From this view, you can use the Animation Effects toolbar, but the Custom Animations feature is not available. Also, titles cannot be animated in this view.

1. From slide sorter view, press Ctrl+A to select all slides (or hold down the Shift key while you click on all the slides that contain text you want to animate).

2. Click one of the Animation Effects buttons (display Animation Effects toolbar if not in view).

3. Click the Text Preset Animation box/choose how text will appear.

**Custom Slide
Show**

If you have a presentation that you want to produce a condensed version of, you won't have to create another file. You can create a Custom Show.

1. From slide view, click Slide Show/Custom Shows/New/name the show in the Name box.

2. Select the slides you want to add to the Custom Show/Add/OK/Show (to see the show)/Close.

To view the Custom Show later:

1. Click Slide Show/Custom Shows/pick show/Show.

Multimedia Presentation

With PowerPoint, you can turn your slide show into a multimedia presentation with movies, music, or your own narration. You can set PowerPoint to play sounds and music automatically or at your command.

Inserting a Media Object

1. In slide view, click Insert/point to Movies and Sounds/click Movie from Gallery to locate movies that come with the software, or click Movie from File to locate a file you have saved (or choose Sound).

Note: *Your Microsoft Office CD-ROM contains a folder called Valupack that contains a collection of sounds, templates, and more.*

Playing an Object

You can play the embedded object while in slide view.

1. Double-click the object to start play.

2. Right-click the object to stop it, or press Esc.

Note: *To make the object play in a slide show, you have to set the play options. We'll do this next.*

POWERPOINT

Playing Movies and Sound in a Slide Show

To change how an embedded movie or sound will play during a Slide Show, you'll need to set the play options.

1. In slide view, right-click on the embedded object/click Custom Animation. You can then set the Timing, Effects, and Play Settings. (**You have to repeat the same steps for each embedded object.**)

Timing

Timing instructs PowerPoint as to when and in what order animation will start for each embedded object. There are two objects embedded on this slide.

- Media 1 is music.
- Media 2 is a movie of a steaming coffee cup.

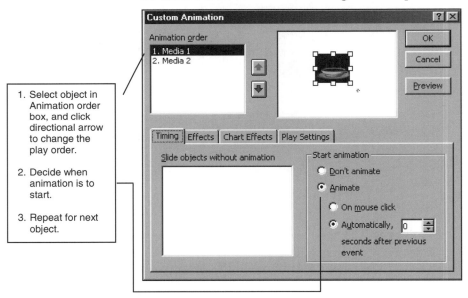

1. Select object in Animation order box, and click directional arrow to change the play order.

2. Decide when animation is to start.

3. Repeat for next object.

With this setup, the animation for the coffee cup and the music was set to start automatically. So, the coffee cup will steam and the music will play simultaneously. Now it's time to change the Effects.

Effects

Change how the object makes its entrance with Effects, then change the Play Settings.

1. Click the Effects tab/make selections/Preview/OK.

Play Settings

Changing the play settings of a media object tells PowerPoint to play it during a slide show.

1. Right-click the object/click Custom Animation/click the Play Settings tab.

2. Click Play using animation order/Continue slide show/Stop playing after current slide.

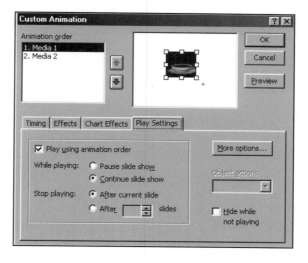

Here, the animation will play in the order indicated, and the slide show will continue while the movie is playing. The movie will stop playing after the current slide.

Note: *Check the Hide while not playing check box only when you don't want a media object to show during the slide show.*

3. Now click the More options button to set the Play Options.

Play Options

Play Options set the way the object plays back.

1. Right-click the object/click Edit Movie Object. (The "More options" button on the Custom Animation dialog box also takes you to the Play Options dialog box.)

Here, the movie will loop and replay until stopped. Now you can play your movie, your music, and your narration during a slide show.

Inserting Narration

You can add voice narration or external sound to your presentation if your computer has a sound card and a microphone. Once inserted, you have to set the timing, play settings, and play options as earlier described.

1. From slide view, click Insert/point to Movies and Sounds/click Record Sound. The Record Sound dialog box appears.

2. Give the sound a name in the Name text box/click the Record button (red circle) /speak into the microphone/click Stop (black square)/click the Play button (black forward arrow) /OK/set options.

Animating a Chart

You can insert a Microsoft Graph and animate it.

1. Click the Insert Chart toolbar button/make changes to the datasheet and watch the changes occur in the chart/close datasheet when finished.

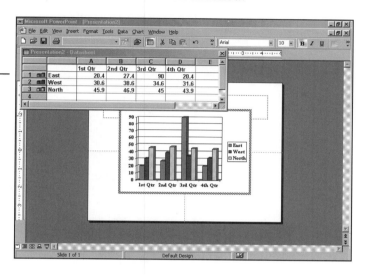

2. Right-click the chart/click Custom Animation.

3. Click the Chart Effects tab/choose how you want chart elements to appear and the entry animation and sound.

4. Click the Timing tab/choose when you want animation to start/click OK.

5. Click off the chart to deselect it.

Note: The Excel chapter has more detail on chart elements. Also, beginning on page 165, you'll learn how to Ungroup and Regroup objects. This will come in handy if you need to have individual chart elements animate independently.

Self-Navigating Show

You can set your slide show up to run continuously on its own.

1. Click Slide Show/Set Up Show (or click Shift+Slide Show button).

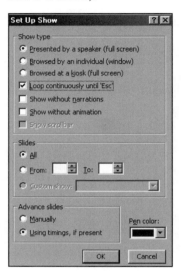

This slide show will loop continuously until stopped and slides will advance using timings you set easier. Press Esc to stop the show.

Rehearse Timing

You can rehearse your timing for a presentation.

1. Go to Slide Sorter view, and select the first slide.
2. Click the Rehearse Timings toolbar button.
3. Rehearse your presentation by using the directional keys on the screen.
4. Press Esc when finished.

Action Buttons

Action buttons help you navigate to various slides during the slide show. The buttons come with PowerPoint and include actions such as Home, Back, Next, etc.

1. From Master view, click AutoShapes on the Drawing toolbar/point to Action Buttons/choose the Home button.

2. Hold down the left mouse button, and drag to create a button.

3. The Action Settings dialog box appears once you release the mouse.

4. The Hyperlink to First Slide option (home page) is already selected, so click OK.

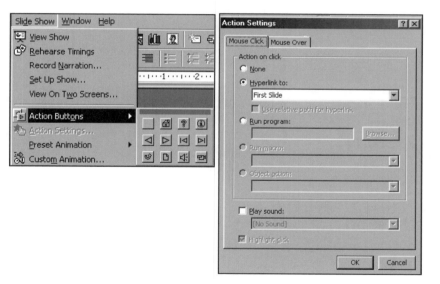

Note: *The Home Action Button was placed on the Master Slide so it would appear on every slide.*

Deleting Objects

1. Click on the object/press the Delete key.

Navigating During Slide Show

To find a particular slide during a slide show:

1. Right-click anywhere on the screen during the show.
2. Point to Go/point to By Title/click desired slide.

Or

1. Type the slide number if you know it, and press Enter.

Or

1. Press Backspace or P to go to the previous slide.
2. Press Enter, Spacebar, or type N to go to the next slide.

Hide Show When Speaking

When you're talking and not referring to the screen:

1. Turn the page black by pressing B, or turn it white by pressing W.
2. Press B or W again to turn the presentation back on.

Notes on Screen During Slide Show

If you need to make markings on the screen during your presentation:

1. Right-click anywhere on the screen during your presentation/click Pen.
2. Mark directly on the screen.

Press E to erase all markings.

OTHER TOPICS

Editing Clip Art

Once Clip Art is embedded, you can break it apart (Ungroup) and use pieces of it, recolor it, crop it, resize it, and duplicate portions of it.

1. In slide view, right-click the graphic/point to Grouping/click Ungroup.

2. Click "Yes to convert the imported object to a Microsoft Office drawing."

3. Click anywhere off the object to clear selection boxes.

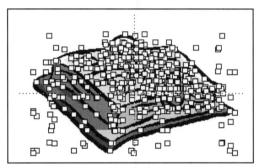

4. Right-click on the pieces to see if they can be ungrouped even more.

Recoloring Clip Art

Once Clip Art is Ungrouped and converted to a Microsoft Drawing object, you can recolor it using the Fill Color tool on the Drawing toolbar.

1. Select the piece of the Ungrouped graphic that needs recoloring/click the Fill Color tool drop-down arrow/make desired color selection.

Once you make desired changes, you'll have to regroup the object (page 166).

POWERPOINT

Regrouping an Object

If you have ungrouped an object and need to regroup it:

1. In slide view, click the Select Objects tool (thick, white arrow on the Drawing toolbar), and draw a selection box around all objects to be regrouped. You must include the entire object inside the selection box in order for it to become selected.

> The selection box is almost imaginary. It disappears once it's done its job of selecting objects.

2. Once the art is selected, right-click it/point to Grouping/click Regroup.

Duplicating Objects

You can duplicate a graphic or drawing object by selecting it and pressing Ctrl+D. You could start with a graphic with a few people in it and create a crowd.

1. In slide view, ungroup the art/duplicate the piece you want by selecting it and pressing Ctrl+D.

2. Drag one of the objects to its new location, and regroup the pieces if needed.

Spacing Objects

You can create even spaces between objects as you duplicate them.

1. In slide view, select the object you want to duplicate/press Ctrl+D.

2. Drag the second object the desired distance from the first object/press Ctrl+D (while the second object is still selected).

3. Continue to press Ctrl+D to create more duplicates, and see how each one is placed the exact distance from each other as the second one was from the first.

Aligning or Distributing Objects

There are several ways to align objects. You can align them with other objects, such as when you align any edge of objects. You can align objects in relation to the entire slide. You can also arrange (or distribute) objects so they are equal distances from each other either vertically or horizontally, or in relation to the entire slide.

1. Select the objects you want to align or distribute/click Draw on the Drawing toolbar/point to Align or Distribute/click your choice.

Guides

You can also align objects by using guides to align them visually.

1. Click View/Guides/click and drag the guides as desired. To get the precise measurement of the distance between objects, hold down the Shift key as you drag the guide between them.

POWERPOINT

Grid

A grid is an invisible matrix used to align objects automatically. If you have Grid on as you draw or move objects, their corners will align at the nearest intersection of the grid (called snap to grid). To turn Grid on or off:

1. Click Draw on the Drawing toolbar/click Grid.

Flipping an Object

You can create a mirror image of an imported object by duplicating it, converting it to a Microsoft Office drawing, and flipping it around.

1. In slide view, click the graphic you want to duplicate/ press Ctrl+D/drag the two graphics apart.
2. Right-click the graphic you want to flip/point to Group/click Ungroup.
3. Click "Yes to convert the object to a Microsoft Office drawing."

You now have to Regroup the object.

4. Draw a selection box around the object/right-click it/point to Group/click Regroup.
5. With the graphic selected, click Draw/point to Rotate or Flip/flip horizontally or vertically.

Rotating an Object

As explained in Flipping an Object, you will have to convert your graphic to a Microsoft Office Drawing.

1. In slide view, select the drawing (or object you converted into a drawing).

2. Click the Free Rotate tool on the Drawing toolbar (the cursor changes into a rotate cursor, and the sizing handles on the object change to green circles).

3. Move the tip of the rotate cursor over one of the green circles, and drag in a circular motion. Press Esc when finished.

Cropping

You can crop or trim portions of a picture. You must be in slide view.

1. Right-click on your object/click Show Picture Toolbar.

2. Click the Crop toolbar button located on the Picture toolbar.

3. Position the cropping tool over a sizing handle (one of the squares surrounding the object), and drag. Press Esc or click off the object when finished.

Tips on Presenting

- Spend more time planning your presentation than creating it.

- The medium is not the message. Don't get caught up in the technology and lose sight of your message.

- Simple is better. Use the same slide transitions and bullet/text animation throughout.

- Enhance your presentation with *simple* graphics on about every 4th slide.

- Text size should be no smaller than 18 pts for readability at a distance.

POWERPOINT

- Keep text to six lines per slide, and six words per line.
- Use no more than three typefaces per slide (logo type doesn't count).
- Do not overuse all caps. The human eye is accustomed to going up and down when reading.
- Do not right justify. It creates too much white space between words and tires the reader.
- Use the professionally-designed color schemes that come with the software.
- Spell check to maintain credibility. If words are wrong, audience won't trust your numbers.
- Use dark background and bright text if preparing on-screen show or 35 mm slides.
- Use light background and dark text for transparencies.
- Spend no more than 2-3 minutes presenting each slide.
- During offline discussions, blacken or whiten the screen or turn machine off.
- **Always** take a backup (i.e., transparencies as a backup to computer slide show).
- Videotape your performance to improve techniques.
- Interject humor as appropriate to keep presentation lively.

Just Show Me
Which Button
to Click!

WINDOWS® 98

GETTING STARTED

If you have no previous experience with Windows, take some time to go through the tutorial available on your Windows CD-ROM. Please note that these instructions may vary depending on which version of Windows you have.

1. Put your Windows CD into your CD-ROM drive.
2. Click the Start button, and then click Run.
3. In the Open box, type tour98, and click OK.
4. Click the tutorial level appropriate for you.

Terminology

- **Windows Desktop**. The screen you see when you start Windows.

- **Icon**. Small pictures on the Desktop that represent a folder with files in it or a program you can use to get your work done.

- **Start Button**. Use to navigate through Windows.

- **Taskbar**. Bar located on your screen with the Start button. The buttons on the task bar indicate which programs are open. Clicking the Minimize Window button in your software sends the program or document to the taskbar. Clicking the program name on the taskbar will bring it into full view on your screen.

- **Click**. Click the mouse button on the left side of the traditional mouse.

- **Right-Click**. Click the button on the right side of the traditional mouse.

- **Double-Click**. Click the left mouse button twice and quickly.

- **Drag**. Press and hold the mouse button as you move the item with the mouse pointer.

- **Ctrl+something**. Press and hold down the Ctrl key and the other item at the same time.

- **Select**. Highlight the item in order to do something with it. The Word chapter has details on how to select.

Windows Update

If you have access to the Internet, this feature will take you to the Microsoft Web site for updates on your software.

1. Click the Start button/click Windows Update/connect to the Internet.

Window Control Buttons

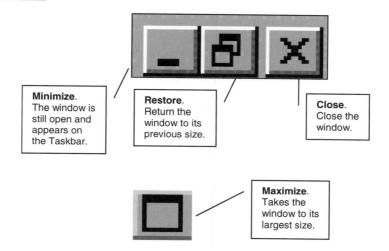

Minimize. The window is still open and appears on the Taskbar.

Restore. Return the window to its previous size.

Close. Close the window.

Maximize. Takes the window to its largest size.

Help in Windows

To get help on the features mentioned in this book:

1. Click the Start button/click Help/click the Index tab/type a keyword/double-click it when you find it.
2. Close Help by clicking the X in the top, right corner.

WINDOWS

HOW IT WORKS

Opening a Program

1. Click the Start button, and point to Programs.

2. Click your selection to open it.

3. **Or**, double-click the program's icon on the Windows Desktop if available.

Opening a Document

1. Click the Start button, and point to Documents (the last 15 documents appear).

2. Point to your selection, and click it.

3. **Or**, click Start, then click Open Office Document.

Adding to the Start Menu

If there is a document or folder you access often, you can add it to the Start Menu (so when you click the Start button, it will be in the list).

1. Right-click the Start button/click Explore.

2. Find folder, document, or program you want to add to Start Menu, and click and drag it to the Start button/release the mouse button to drop it.

Opening Program When Windows Opens

If you always want a program that you want to open when Windows opens (i.e., your calendar), you can add it to the Start Menu StartUp.

1. Right-click the Start button/click Explore.

2. Go to the Windows folder/double-click Start Menu.

3. Click the **+** sign next to Programs/double-click StartUp/click the program you want, and drag it to the right side of the window, and drop it.

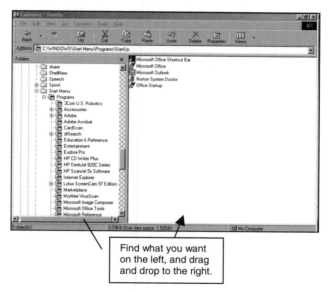

Find what you want on the left, and drag and drop to the right.

Removing from StartUp

You can remove programs or folders from StartUp at any time.

1. Click the Start button.

2. Point to Settings, and click Taskbar & Start Menu.

3. Click the Start Menu Programs tab.

4. Click Add or Remove, and follow prompts.

WINDOWS

Creating Shortcuts

Creating a shortcut to a file (or program) on the Windows Desktop. Once the shortcut is created, you can double-click it and open the file or program right from the Desktop.

1. Right-click the Start button.
2. Click Explore.
3. Click the Restore button if you can't see the Windows Desktop (see the Restore button in the Window Control Buttons section on page 175.)
4. Find the file you want a shortcut to.
5. Right-click the file name, and while holding down the right mouse button, drag it to the Windows Desktop/release the mouse button.
6. Click Copy Here or Create Shortcut(s) Here.

Copying or Moving Files

To a diskette:

1. Put a diskette into your A: drive.
2. Right-click the Start button.
3. Click Explore.
4. Find the file you want to copy, and right-click it.
5. Point to Send To, then click 3 1/2 floppy (A).

From diskette to hard drive or to another folder (copying or moving):

1. Right-click the Start button/click Explore.
2. Find the file you want to copy or move/right-click it, and drag the file to its new folder location/release the mouse button/choose Copy or Move.

   Or, right-click the file/click the Copy toolbar button/find the new folder, and double-click it to open/click the Paste toolbar button.

Note: See more information on moving files on page 184.

Copying / Formatting a Disk

1. Double-click the My Computer icon on the Windows Desktop.
2. Right-click 3 1/2 floppy (A).
3. Click Copy Disk (or Format), and follow prompts.

Deleting Files

1. Right-click the Start button/click Explore.
2. Find what you want to delete/click it/press the Delete key.

Recycle Bin

Deleted files remain on your hard drive until you empty the Recycle Bin.

WINDOWS

Emptying Recycle Bin

1. Double-click the Recycle Bin icon (on your Windows Desktop) to open it.

2. Click File, then click Empty Recycle Bin.

Note: To bypass the Recycle Bin when deleting a file, follow instructions for deleting files on page 179, but press and hold down the Shift key before you press Delete.

Restoring Deleted Files

Files that are in the Recycle Bin can be restored to your hard drive.

1. Double-click the Recycle Bin icon (on your Windows Desktop) to open it.

2. Right-click the desired file/click Restore.

Renaming Files

1. Right-click the Start button.

2. Click Explore.

3. Find the file to rename, and click on the file name. Wait a second, and click it again. A box should appear around the file name. (**Or**, right-click on the file name, and click Rename.)

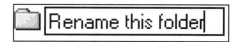

Type the new file name (inside the box) /press Enter (or click anywhere off the name).

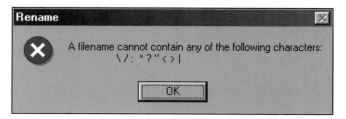

Adding to the Office Shortcut Bar

This is the toolbar with program/file icons located on the Windows Desktop (if installed with Microsoft Office).

Adding programs or files to it:

1. Right-click the background (a space that has no button) on Shortcut Bar/click Customize.
2. Click the Buttons tab, and click desired selection(s).

Or:

1. Right-click the Start button.
2. Click Explore.
3. Find what you want to add/click and drag it to the Shortcut Bar/release the mouse button.

Creating a Computer Filing System

Organizing your folders on the computer makes it easier to find what you need.

Before you get started, make an outline of how you want your computer filing system to look. First, it will help to understand how a good, logical filing system is set up.

Tips on Setting Up a Good Filing System

A filing system should be logical so there is never any doubt where you might have filed something.

Take your job description or business plan and break it down, beginning with broad, main categories. Use nouns for each category. Subcategorize the main categories, then continue to break the subjects down further if needed.

WINDOWS

Filing System Example

Start with the broadest category and work your way down.

Business (First category under My Documents. On this same level, you might have a folder for Personal.)

   Marketing (subcategory of Business)

      Advertisements
      Networking
            (Create folder for each networking group)
      Public Relations
            Media Campaigns
                  Contest
            Media Kit
            The Media
                  Print
                  Radio
                  TV
      Seminars
      Web Page

Note: *Visit my Web site at www.duncanresource.com for more details on how to develop a good, logical filing system.*

Once the filing system is created, you will need to create new folders on your computer for each category. If you have been up and running for awhile and you have all your documents clumped together in one folder, you will need to drag them to the new folders.

Creating New Folders

This is how the computer filing system will be created.

1. Right-click the Start button/click Explore/find the My Documents folder/double-click it to open.

2. Click File, point to New, then click Folder.

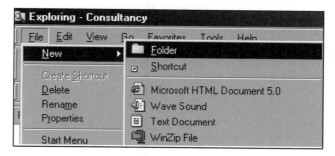

3. Type the name "Business" for the new folder (on the right-side of the window), and press Enter. The new folder becomes a subfolder of My Documents.

Creating Subfolders

To create a subfolder, *you have to make sure you have the right folder open*. The open folder is indicated on the Address line. To create a subfolder of the Business folder, double-click it to open it first, then create the subfolder.

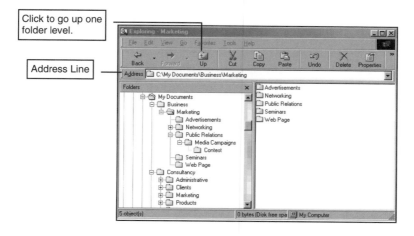

Moving to new folders

If you have dumped all your files into the My Documents folder, you will have to move all the files into the new folders.

1. Double-click the My Documents folder so all the files you have created are on the right-hand side of the window.

2. On the left-hand side of the window, find your main folder (My Documents) and **click** (one click) **all** the plus signs next to **all** of its subfolders so **all** folders and subfolders belonging to My Documents are in view on the left-hand side.

3. Click a file on the right, and drag it to its appropriate folder on the left side of the window. The highlighted folder is the one in which the file will relocate to.

   ▤ If there are adjacent files you need to move to the same folder, click on the first file, and while holding down the Shift key, click on the last file in the group. All the files in the group will become selected.

   ▤ If you see files in nonadjacent locations you need to move to the same folder, click each file while holding down the Ctrl key. Each file will become selected.

   If you need to deselect a file, continue holding down the Ctrl key, and click on the file again.

   ▤ If you need to glance at a file before you move it, right-click on it, and click Quick View (if installed).

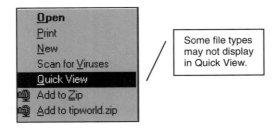

Some file types may not display in Quick View.

Finding Files

1. Right-click the Start button, and click Find.

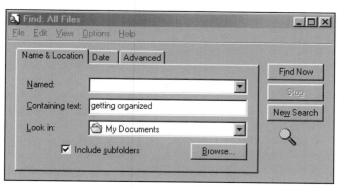

2. If you want to look for all files containing certain text, type the text in the Containing text box.

3. If you know the name of the folder or file, type it in the **Named** text box/click the **Look in** drop-down arrow (or click the Browse button) to instruct Windows where to look for the file/click Find Now.

   If you know a part of the file name, type it, and use the * as a wildcard. For example, organi* will look for all files with these letters in the name.

4. If what you're looking for pops up before the system has finished looking, click Stop/double-click the folder or file to open.

Note: *To narrow the search, complete information behind the Date and Advanced tabs before clicking Find Now.*

Customizing the Windows Desktop

1. Right-click on empty space anywhere on the Windows Desktop.

2. Click Properties, and make desired changes.

WINDOWS

WORD INDEX

WORD

WORD

EXCEL INDEX

EXCEL

POWERPOINT INDEX

POWERPOINT

WINDOWS INDEX

WINDOWS

Suggested Reading

Just Show Me Which Button to Click! "Computer Training for Busy People" will get you so comfortable with your software that you'll be ready to tackle those big, thick books. But this time, you won't feel overwhelmed or intimidated!

From QUE® Corporation

    Using series.

From Microsoft® Press

    Running series.

About the Author

PEGGY DUNCAN, CEO
Duncan Resource Group, Inc.
Efficiency Consulting
Organization-Time Management-Technology

Peggy Duncan provides consulting services to businesses looking to make work easier for their staff and to individuals seeking to increase their efficiency. By providing her clients with the tools they need to get organized, streamline business processes, and make better use of technology, Peggy not only gives her clients a competitive edge, but helps them free up time to enjoy their lives more fully.

After graduating from Atlanta Junior College (now Atlanta Metropolitan College) with an A.S. degree in Business Administration and from Georgia State University with a B.S. degree in Marketing, the Durham, NC native began a corporate career at IBM. Throughout her stay at IBM, Peggy received numerous awards for developing more efficient processes and procedures.

After IBM, Peggy worked for Georgia-Pacific Corporation, where she developed most of her training and software skills. While there, she received a Train the Trainer certificate from Georgia State University.

Peggy is a columnist with the *Atlanta Tribune* and *the Network Journal* of New York City, and the former software specialist and host of the Atlanta cable TV show, *TECHsupport*. She has been written about in the *Atlanta Business Chronicle*, the *Atlanta Journal-Constitution*, the *Carolina Times*, the *Triangle Tribune*, and *Good News* magazine. Peggy has been featured on www.officedepot.com and www.blackenterprise.com.

Partial Client List: Georgia-Pacific Corporation, Georgia Power, Mead Containerboard, Q-Time Restaurant, The New York Times Regional Newspaper Group, Southern Polytechnic State, Georgia Tech.

Memberships: The Atlanta Business League, Atlanta Hispanic Chamber of Commerce, National Association of Women Business Owners, Society for Human Resource Management, Georgia Speakers Association.

Computer Classes

This book makes learning this software easy. However, some of you may still want an instructor-led class. Classes based on this book can be arranged at your company site. The class, like the book, focuses on beginning to advanced features that will save you the most time.

Prerequisite: Prior Windows knowledge (Windows training also available).

Word	4 hours, Beginning to Advanced
Excel	4 Hours, Beginning to some Advanced
PowerPoint	4 Hours, Beginning to Advanced
Special-Word Power User	4 hours, More Advanced Learning

Note: It is strongly recommended that the client follow a format allowing no more than four hours of training per day.

Regardless of skill levels, students learn many little-known, timesaving tips buried in this software (so don't worry about mixing skill levels within the class). People that have used this software for years are just as amazed by it as the newer users. Remember, 80% of the people still use the computer like it's a typewriter.

What sets this training apart from the rest? The training is quick and fun. We've cut out all the fat but not the meat, just showing you which buttons to click! Also, we don't repeat features in Excel or PowerPoint that you've already learned in Word, just like in the book.

Also, Peggy is a former Documentation Specialist. She has had to use this software to create very complex training manuals with non-negotiable deadlines. She hasn't just learned a script for a class. She wrote the book from her real-world experience. She knows the features that will excite you and that you'll need every day. That's what her classes (and this book) are all about.

ORDER MORE COPIES OF THIS BOOK

Without damaging the book, please photocopy the order form below, complete it, and mail it with your payment, or fax with your credit card information, to the address (or fax number) below. Please make checks payable and mail to:

PSC Press
1010 Pine Tree Trail, Suite 300, Atlanta GA 30349-4979
TEL 770-991-1316 FAX 770-907-4438
Or order online at www.amazon.com or www.fatbrain.com.

Our Price (U.S.)	$24.99 for 1 book; 2-4 books=$19.99ea; 5-99 books=$14.99ea.
Shipping	$3 for first book. $1 for each additional book. Usually ships in 24 hrs.
Volume Orders	Bookstores, distributors, wholesalers, libraries, schools, corporations, government agencies, and other volume buyers, please call the publisher directly for special discounts. Or send an eMail to pscpress@mindspring.com, and indicate in the subject line which of the above categories you fall under. We will send you a copy of our Discount Schedule, Terms and Conditions, and Return Policy. Sorry, but no consignment orders are accepted. Thank you.

QUANTITY _____ **Just show me which button to click!**

Print Name

First   MI   Last

Street Address

                                                      Apt/Suite
City / State / Zip

City   ST   Zip

Phone/Fax/eMail   (   )   (   )

Phone   FAX
eMail:

Credit Card Info   Name as on the card
☐ Visa ☐ MC
☐ Disc ☐ AX   Account No.

          Expiration Date

          Your Signature

Mail or fax to PSC Press, 1010 Pine Tree Trail, Suite 300, Atlanta GA 30349.
TEL 770-991-1316   Fax 770-907-4438.

Total Sale

_____ # of bks
X $ PRICE
= $ _____
GA Tax $ _____
(7%)   (GA residents)
+Shpg $ _____
Total $ _____

Thank You!